NEVER TOO THIN

NEVER TOO THIN

By

ÉVA SZÉKELY

The Women's Press

In memory of my grandparents:

Glaub Fáni (1892-1944),
Klein Jenő József (1889-1944),
Moskovits Miklós (1899-1944),
Weisz Erzsébet (1906-1944)

CANADIAN CATALOGUING IN PUBLICATION DATA
Szekely, Eva Aniko
Never too thin—

Includes bibliographical references.
ISBN 0-88961-127-0

1. Anorexia nervosa — Social aspects. 2. Bulimia —
Social aspects. 3. Women — Socialization.
4. Leanness — Psychological aspects. I. Title.

RC552.A5S94 1988   305.4   C88-094828-0

Cover art: Jan Thornhill
Cover design: Linda Gustafson
Editor: Ann Decter
Copy Editor: Ellen Quigley
Proofreader: Pinelopi Gramatikopoulos

Printed and bound in Canada

Published by
The Women's Press
229 College Street No. 204
Toronto, Ontario M5T 1R4

This book was produced by
the collective effort of The Women's Press.
This book was the project of
the Social Issues Group.

The Women's Press gratefully acknowledges
financial support from The Canada Council
and the Ontario Arts Council

To return to the things themselves is to return to that world which precedes knowledge, of which knowledge always *speaks*, and in relation to which every scientific schematization is an abstract and derivative sign-language, as is geography in relation to the countryside in which we have learnt beforehand what a forest, a prairie or a river is.

Merleau-Ponty,
Phenomenology of Perception

Looking for the world's essence is not looking for an idea reduced to a theme of discourse; it is looking for what it is as a fact for us, before any thematization.

Merleau-Ponty,
Phenomenology of Perception

CONTENTS

ACKNOWLEDGEMENTS

I would like to acknowledge the contributions of the women interviewed for this study, who generously shared their lives with me and contributed their experiences to help me explicate the pursuit of thinness among women. Many friends, colleagues and former teachers encouraged me to write this book and gave their support through various phases of this research. I am particularly grateful to Kathleen Rockhill, Dorothy E. Smith and Frances Tolnai for discussions of earlier drafts. Charis Wahl suggested a new format for restructuring the manuscript. I am grateful to the collective of The Women's Press for their interest in this topic, and especially to Maureen FitzGerald for all the work she has done to make this book possible. The final version of this work would have been most difficult to complete without Ann Decter; I greatly enjoyed her thinking along with me as she helped reorganize the material and clarify ideas. I greatly appreciate Ellen Quigley's thorough work in copy-editing the final draft. From the very beginning to the very end of this project, Douglas Bors has been a solidly supportive and loving partner. His questions, constructively critical comments and his belief in the importance of my research sustained me in moments of doubt and fatigue.

Work on parts of this book was supported by grants from the Ontario Arts Council and from the Social Sciences and Humanities Research Council of Canada.

INTRODUCTION

"I always wanted you to admire my fasting," said the hunger artist.... "But you shouldn't admire it".... "Because I have to fast, I can't help it" .... "Because, ... because I couldn't find the food I liked. If I had found it, believe me, I should have made no fuss and stuffed myself like you or anyone else." (Kafka 1971, 277)

The hunger artist lived most of his life in a cage. Daily, for years, people flocked to his cage, and, openmouthed, they stood marvelling at his skeletonlike figure and sunken eyes. He was an attraction for a while, then forgotten; the zoo keepers no longer bothered marking the number of days he spent fasting. He spoke the above words just before he died, when someone suddenly remembered to ask who was in that cage next to those of the animals behind the circus.

I, too, marvelled when I first saw a skeletonlike woman during a psychiatry round in one of the local hospitals. The chair in which she sat looked oversized relative to her body. Her eyes were sunken, the bones of her face were visible, her ribs and hip bones showed through the thick sweat suit she wore. She reminded me of a frightened, freezing, hungry bird. I wondered what it was that she wanted but could not have. I knew it was not food. I suspect it was not food that the hunger artist wanted, either. But what did the woman want?

In the following months I was asked to conduct psychological assessments of several women (and one man) who were diagnosed as anorexic and/or bulimic. I never quite found out what each of them wanted and could not have. I did not understand them. I could not make sense — except at a level that was too abstract to be directly relevant to my purposes — of how they could say and do what they did. Some of them cooked and baked for others, but ate none of the food themselves. Others ate in secret, consumed huge amounts of food that they immediately attempted to purge to avoid gaining weight. Yet others insisted they should lose another five, ten or more pounds when they already looked as if they barely had the strength to walk.

I was baffled. They were all young, white and educated, and, with one exception, they were all women. Some came from various cultural backgrounds, some were working class and others middle or upper-middle class. I seemed unable to find a common ground that might help me grasp their plights. The only substantial difference I could see between me and the women with whom I worked was that, unlike them, I did not grow up in North America. The realization of this difference led me to explore sociocultural issues relevant to the lives of these women.

Impatiently, I began to pore over the psychological literature on eating disorders. I came across several pieces of writing that suggested that anorexia nervosa and bulimia were "new diseases" (Bruch 1979, vii), that they were the "sociocultural epidemic" of our time (Garner et al. 1980, 484). There were clear suggestions that, in addition to the individual and family factors, sociocultural factors were also contributing to the apparent increase in the prevalence of these eating disorders.

Discussions of the sociocultural factors centred on the shifting cultural ideals toward thinner and more angular shapes for women since the mid-1960s, society's preoccupation with youth, fitness, fashion and dieting and the changing roles of women in recent decades (Garner et al. 1980; Palazzoli 1974; Wooley & Wooley 1982). This has helped me to locate some of the possible sources for the statements and actions of my patients. Most writings, however, did not detail, concretely, the day-to-day issues, actions and concerns of the anorexic and bulimic women to the sociocultural structures in which we live.

It was the recognition of this gap between the everyday lives of persons with eating disorders and the sociocultural factors as discussed by the literature that gave rise to the research. I wanted to elucidate more fully the mundane, both the daily experiences and actions of anorexic and bulimic women and the inter-relationships of their experiences with the sociocultural context of their lives. I decided to study white women only, because, according to the demographic information, the overwhelming majority of these patients are women (Palmer 1983, 15), and 97 percent of these women are white (Levenkron 1982, 1). I wanted to discern from the everyday life experiences of anorexic and bulimic women the specific goals, aspirations, values, norms, images, ideals and expectations by which they have lived, as well as to begin to uncover the ways in which these values, norms, ideals and expectations are socially and culturally constituted.

By values, norms, ideals and goals, I do not mean objectives consciously formulated or wilfully decided upon by women. Instead, I understand these to be tacitly lived through constit-uents or dimensions around which our activities are organized. They are that which we try to bring into existence in our actions, including our thoughts, wishes, fantasies. They are embedded in our particular social situations, and these situations both shape and are shaped by our actions. Values, goals, ideals and aspira-tions are neither completely given nor completely the makings of individuals' separate lives. Values are abstractions from social conditions that both condition us and are conditioned by us. Valued ways to live or valued things to have may become the foci (whether they are reflected upon or not) that channel our actions. These activities stem from certain motives based on needs, which are also socially conditioned (Lomov 1982). Thus, an analysis of the sociocultural dimensions of the "relentless pursuit of excessive thinness" (Bruch 1979, ix) among women would have to include the uncovering of socially constituted needs that may be taken up in activities toward certain goals.

I became interested in the question of goals, values, norms and aspirations as I began to be aware of what I felt was missing from the lives of women whose activities seemed so very focused on the pursuit of thinness. In part, because of my having been brought up in a society quite different from North America, I learned another set of valued ways to live. For me, work has been very important, especially work that seemed to have the promise of making the world a better place to live. By "better" I mean more just, more fair, more egalitarian, more communal and humane. Since my teens I have called this "worthwhile work." Most of the women I interviewed did not feel their work was intrinsically worthwhile or meaningful.

During my first twenty years in Hungary, I also learned that goals and means had to be realistic. Impossible ideals were relegated to the realm of fantasy and had to be recognized as such. Several of the women who had problems with anorexia nervosa or bulimia seemed to chase dreams or, at best, ideals that could never be actualities. They seemed to know very little about the world outside patriarchally defined women's roles, and, in general, their lives appeared to me almost exclusively focused on their individual happiness. The interviewed women's notion of independence seemed to boil down to their control of the body, of their appearance.

These differences between my life and that of the women with whom I worked served as openings toward an exploration of the social dimensions of the relentless pursuit of thinness. The differences in the social contexts are not causes of eating disorders. Rather, the grounds or contexts of people's lives shape possible activities. My original research became complicated by several factors.

First, I began to wonder whether hospitalized patients could provide the type of description I needed to gain access to the sociocultural contexts of their everyday lives. What made me ask this question was that they all seemed eager to talk about their hospital experiences, but not about their lives prior to hospitalization. Further, many of them were on medication that made it difficult for them to concentrate for long periods of time. As I was making these observations, I gradually moved toward wanting to interview non-hospitalized, recovering or recovered anorexic and bulimic women.

Second, as I was discussing the topic of my research with colleagues and acquaintances I was surprised by the manner in which anorexia nervosa and bulimia struck a chord of interest among all the women. Especially when I used the phrase "the relentless pursuit of thinness," many of them talked spontaneously about their own experiences in the pursuit of thinness. I noted with surprise that several of them described their experiences in much the same words as the hospitalized women. One colleague said she felt best about herself when she weighed 105 pounds (her lowest adult weight ever), and now, being heavier than that, she really despised herself. I saw her as a very attractive and not at all fat woman, and I could not grasp how being ten or fifteen pounds heavier would make such a difference in the way she felt about herself. Other similar incidents led me to think that I needed to broaden the scope of my investigation to include women who were not diagnosed as anorexic and/or bulimic and who were not necessarily hospitalized.

Third, I discovered that I, too, have participated in and perpetuated the ideological use of the concepts "eating disorders," "anorexia nervosa" and "bulimia." When a concept is used ideologically, subjects and relations between subjects — precisely that which needs to be understood — disappear. We start with concepts as if we were on the outside, detached from the very relationships and practices that produce them. These concepts, their origin, construction and place in a network of relationships and practices, are not questioned; they are treated as if we already understand them:

> To think ideologically ... is to proceed so as to remain "on this side of" the concept, to rupture the internal relation in the observable between concept and "what men actually do." Concepts then become a boundary to enquiry rather than a beginning. How it is possible for us to think these things and to talk about these things is excluded as topic. Used ideologically, the concept confines the

thinker *within* the conditions of his experience since these are already taken for granted in the currency in which he thinks. Thus to think ideologically is indeed to be determined situationally. (Smith 1974, 44)

Once I realized that my ideological use of a concept limited *a priori* the possibilities of understanding the phenomenon, I was impelled to open up the fundamental themes and questions that have organized my proposed research. By not starting with what women who want to be thin actually do in a given context, practices and their interrelationships may become concealed, and we may simply reiterate what we already know or think we know.

As an apprentice in a helping profession, I have been exposed to, and asked to participate in, a set of practices that distinguish sharply between pathological and normal, without questioning how those distinctions have developed. I have been steeped in the assumptions of these fields, read the established journals, books, attended conferences and workshops, studied the diagnostic and statistical manuals and tried to understand from the outside, as instructed by the authors, what anorexia nervosa is really about. Gradually, I have realized that to begin to answer this question, I had to reformulate it, starting with what is the pursuit of thinness among women about?

In the process of actually doing this research, it became increasingly evident that thinness was a vehicle, rather than the goal, of women's relentless pursuit of thinness. In striving to produce themselves as attractively thin, they were striving for their very existence. With this observation, my focus shifted further toward an explication of women's situations. The conflicts the women experienced began to point to a host of contradictions in their situations. The relations that started to emerge between the conflicting experiences of the women and the real contradictions in the social world marked yet another shift.

It was not the purpose of this research to address the question of why a particular woman becomes preoccupied with the practices of the relentless pursuit of thinness to the exclusion of other concerns. This is an issue that has been raised by many experts and interested lay persons. Researchers have attempted to investigate family factors while searching for clues about the specific characteristics of women who become victims of the relentless pursuit of thinness (Harkaway 1987; Minuchin, Rosman & Gailer 1978; Yager 1982; Strober 1981). From a feminist perspective, researchers have also taken up this question, focusing primarily on the mother-daughter relationship (Boskind-Lodahl 1976; Orbach 1986). A number of possible explanations have been offered ranging from ego-boundary disturbance (Sugarman, Quinlan & Devenis 1982) through poor impulse control (Halmi 1983) to enmeshed families in which parents are unable to make their daughters eat (Minuchin, Rosman & Gailer 1978) and role conflicts (Dunn & Ondercin 1981) due to women's changing situations in our time. Rost, Neuhaus and Florin (1982) have suggested that the breakdown of traditional sex roles may be one factor in the increasing prevalence of bulimia and anorexia nervosa. According to recent reports in the press, feminism has brought on the shift in cultural values to which women with eating disorders have fallen victim (*The Toronto Star* 13 Nov. 1986, H8). Although each of these explanations may point to certain aspects of women's socially and historically constituted situations, at best they are inadequate answers to the questions: Why women? Why mostly white women? Why almost exclusively in the "have" countries? And why in the last twenty years do we see more and more women pursuing thinness? Women's roles have been changing elsewhere in the world as well, yet women in Eastern Europe and in the developing countries have not been dieting, binging and purging as have women in North America and Western Europe.

My emphasis on the social-historical constitution of the relentless pursuit of thinness is not an attempt to deny the importance of the personal (individual) or the family as contexts of experience. The personal and family are categories in their own right, and they cannot be collapsed completely into the matrix of social relations (Sartre 1963). Women's pursuit of thinness cannot be reduced to social conditioning or to socialization alone; rather, the context is an ever-present dimension of women's lives. This context must be grasped more fully if we are to appreciate the rationality of women's practices. The same practices that Bruch terms a "disease" (1979, vii) — however "amazing" and "awe-inspiring" (ibid., 5) they are — appear to be sensible and even normal. They do not represent a radical departure from the lives of many other women in similar situations or within the lives of the interviewed women themselves when we view the practices in their social-historical contexts.

On the basis of the present research and recent literature on the social class background of women in the relentless pursuit of thinness, the assumption that most women in the relentless pursuit of thinness are upper-middle class or upper class needs to be called into question. The pursuit of thinness now seems to be wide-spread among women of all social classes. The presence of this phenomenon among women of all social classes has to be viewed in light of the media's image-making and compelling function in patriarchal capitalist political-economic structures. Woman's body as a site of domination is subjected to further commodification, objectification and alienation. At the same time, control over the body is the means of resisting domination: the body is a tool to attempt to break out of a certain form of subjugation — in the hope of positioning oneself in less oppressive relationships.

The research presented in this book departs in two important ways from both the clinical and feminist writings. First, in both the clinical and the feminist literature, the relentless pursuit of thinness is discussed as a disease or illness. Second, both approaches treat the individual in a reductive and dualistic manner. The social is conceptualized in the clinical literature merely as a factor. The feminist literature on anorexia has also failed to grasp individual development consistently in social terms. The framework for which I argue is one that recognizes from the beginning that individual existence cannot at any point be treated in isolation from the social. "In everyday life ... we have — and must have — society in our bones" (O'Neill 1985, 24); we carry social relations in our bodies. The body is always *in* society, hence it must be grasped in its concrete existence socially and historically.

The stories of Katrina, Simone, Liz, Judith and Martha (all pseudonyms) demonstrate, beyond any doubt, that the relentless pursuit of thinness, as it is lived in our society today, is bound up intimately with women's having to be attractive to men. The interviewed women have experienced the necessity of being attractive to men in general and have learned that they should seek to attract certain kinds of men — men of status and wealth as depicted in the media. Having to be attractive at this time and in our media-dominated society means unequivocally having to be thin. If a woman is not attractively thin, it becomes increasingly difficult for her to be accepted by any group, to be asked for dates and, subsequently, to be married. It will be harder for her to obtain, keep and be promoted in a job. In North America today, thinness is a precondition for being perceived by others and oneself as healthy. This perception may make all the difference in whether a woman will or will not have a job. Simone's life story does not allow us to forget that a fat woman is an ostracized and penalized woman in this society at the present time.

The life stories presented here suggest that the relentless pursuit of thinness is not a uniform phenomenon. Different life situations and circumstances may lead to the pursuit of thinness, and this pursuit may even be lived in rather varied manners. Yet, the five women did all pursue thinness. The values, ideals, images and aspirations that emerge from their accounts of their lives show great similarities. In interview after interview, certain themes appear regularly: having to be a "good girl" (perfect daughter, date, wife and mother); the necessity of being slim (avoiding being fat) and attractive to men; the requirement of being feminine (ladylike), with all the work it implies (including turning to experts for advice), as well as being smart or bright; the call to stand out (to become successful, rich and famous) and to fit in with peers.

The imperatives to be thin and attractive emerge from these stories as a major part of women's work. It is work to be carried out on a daily basis, every day of a woman's life. We are told constantly that we must diet, exercise (workout), learn about ladylike manners and be knowledgeable about matters of health, fashion and appearance in general. We must compete and become the most attractive of attractive women in order to get and keep men's attention. In seeking to secure men's attention, women's existence undergoes a transformation. It takes on the character of a commodity, an object constantly in need of perfection for men's service and pleasure. As commodities, we can be used and discarded by men — if deemed desirable in the first place.

If we want to prevent harm to women through the relentless pursuit of thinness, we must ask: What in the sociocultural contexts of women's lives has created the possibility and the necessity for women to engage in these practices? What kinds of social relations, in what type of society, provide the conditions for the relentless pursuit of thinness? How do these social relations co-constitute women's practices concerning their bodies?

Parts of the answers to these questions can be found in examining how women's bodies have become a site of domination; how differences between women and men have been emphasized, exaggerated and exploited in ways that have fostered the objectification of women's bodies by both men and women. At present, a woman's body has to be thin, shapely, flexible and fragile-looking (even if it is muscular). Such a body gives the impression of being easy to manipulate as well as in need of protection. The current ideal of femininity fosters a view of woman as childlike and weak, as someone to display, play with and then discard. Desire and pleasure have been commodified; Laura Kipnis' 1985 video, *Ecstasy Unlimited: The Interpenetration of Sex and Capital* demonstrates that sexuality has become the new business for corporate America. Sexual life functions in relation to the needs of profit in the supply side of capitalism, where democracy is defined as freedom to buy the best and equal opportunities in spending.

In such a context, a woman's body becomes further commodified. Her shape and her entire appearance must keep up with the changes in what constitutes objects of fetish and what the buyer — the men of status and wealth — will purchase. Women's strength, joy, work and the varieties of women's physical shape are not celebrated under these conditions.

A striking sign of the domination of women's bodies is that we hardly have a language — words, gestures and movements — to explore and express our bodies in a manner that would enable us to begin to question the taken-for-granted ideals and categories of what women's bodies should be like and what they should be for. The language we use to talk about the body and our concerns about the body is, to a large degree, the language and the images of the popular media. Women typically say that they feel the best (healthiest, happiest, most sexually attractive) when they are thin (as thin as possible); questioning such statements amounts to blasphemy. It is easy to locate the same statements and images in women's magazines, television, advertising, daily papers and how-to books — materials that are virtually omnipresent in our lives.

White women in North America and Western Europe have especially appropriated the ideal of thinness and its corollaries of attractiveness, health, beauty, youth and sexuality with relatively few exceptions. We have learned to relate to our bodies in an objectified manner. We view and treat the body as if from the outside, as if through the eyes of others; these "others" are men.

Our inability to name and describe our bodily experiences also alienates us from our sexuality which might enable us to transform our relationship to the body.

Openings for discourses on women's bodies as a site of domination are few indeed. In the recent past, women have begun to write about their relationships with their mothers (and, to some degree, with other women), but not with their fathers. A few popular writings, for example, Nancy Friday's book, *My Mother/Myself*, have created the spaces for discussions about mothers and daughters, although these books have not challenged radically the status quo within which mother-daughter relationships are formed. Similar spaces, however, have not opened up to bring to surface the ambiguous and often painful feelings and experiences with fathers and men in general. When women's relationships with their fathers, husbands, lovers, colleagues and other men in their lives are written about or discussed in the popular media, the treatment of these issues tends to be sensational. The experiences they address are constructed as extreme acts committed by sick/abnormal or criminal men against other women. The connection is barely made with women's subordination, and no analysis is provided of the social relations in which such acts take place. Typical examples of these "extreme cases" include rape, wife battering and murder, incest and prostitution. What actually constitutes these cases is not clear-cut.

Anorexia nervosa and bulimia have been presented in a manner similar to rape, prostitution and incest: these events are depicted as if they could only happen to other women, as if they were not potential experiences of most women in our society. The difference between the ideological construction of eating disorders and rape, for example, is that, in the case of anorexia nervosa, women's subordination and the social context in which it occurs is rendered more invisible by the classification of anorexia nervosa as an illness. In this regard, anorexia nervosa and bulimia are more similar to the construction and classification of a selected set of women's experiences, such as depression, which then become the domain of psychiatry rather than of general critical social analysis and action (see Stoppard 1988).

But what are women's real possibilities for establishing a sense of the body and self-worth that are not based on appearances? What would it require to create the ground — and what could be the ground? — of a relationship to the body that is not externalized, racist and heterosexist in the conventional sense of being derived from and directed toward the necessity of attracting men? What are the implications of living in nuclear families, in a white media-dominated society, of learning in an educational system that fosters individual achievement, competition and treats girls and boys bodies differently from the start? What transformations in social relations might make it less likely that women will be viewed and consequently view themselves as commodities? These are some of the important questions with which we have to struggle collectively.

Liz, Katrina, Simone, Martha and Judith have largely struggled alone. Their stories speak to a purpose in their lives beyond attempting to make their bodies conform to the current ideal of feminine body. Each of them has tried to make herself tolerated, desired and wanted. Each attempted to hold on to something — something as concrete as her weight or body shape and size. We cannot grasp the essence of this pursuit merely in terms of passive submission to a certain ideal appearance. The practices of the relentless pursuit of thinness point to women's striving to have a sense of worth and control in a situation that is often experienced as almost totally ruled by others. Ultimately, the relentless pursuit of thinness signifies women's struggle for a place in the world.

This struggle is ridden with conflicts and contradictions. The lessons these five women have learned, the images, values and ideals they have sought to actualize, are often at odds with one another. They have appropriated images of perfection, valuing competence and success in all spheres of life, seeking eternal beauty, youth, happiness, health, virtue, irresistible desirability, exemplary living, as well as fun-loving adventure. They also learned that they should be smart, do well at school, study to be a professional (or "anything" she wants to be), but never try to be smarter than a man. To attract men, she should act dumb and pretend to be less competent than him, particularly in domains that have been considered masculine. To be required to be competitive as well as always to care for others are mutually exclusive and impossible ideals. So is independence —women should make their own decisions and take care of their own needs — when learned simultaneously with the virtue of pleasing and obeying their parents/husbands/boyfriends.

Many of these values and images, and the practices they imply, are polar opposites. The inconsistencies in values and ideals point to actual contradictions and conflicts in white North American and Western European society today. Values of co-operation and caring are not compatible with values of competition, individual success and happiness. In the last few decades in North America, women's actual and potential situations have become increasingly contradictory. This issue was raised in several writings on anorexia, where conflicts between fulfilling women's traditional tasks of being mothers and wives as well as living up to the expectation of having careers outside the home have been described. A report by the Canadian Advisory Council on teenage girls in Canada indicates that the aspiration to fulfil this double mission has been internalized by most girls in this country (Baker 1985).

The tension between being a working woman and a mother and wife is real enough. When each of these tasks is presented in a glamourized fashion, the difficulties increase manifold. We will feel like failures if what we have to compare ourselves to are picture-perfect glossy images. It is important to note, however, that even a scaled down version of these images with all their mundane aspects is a realistic aspiration only for a small percentage of women in this country. However desirable or undesirable these practices may be, very few women become successful career women and very few move up in society by marriage.

The women whose lives have been told here are among countless others who are caught in the contradiction between an idealized version of life and our actual everyday reality. It is not the mind of the anorexic that has played tricks on her; she is not thought disordered, or engaged in dichotomous thinking, as many experts have depicted. Rather, she has been tricked by the promises that have been made to women but never delivered. For the survival of this political-economic system, it must continue to make promises to women that foster the belief that we can succeed. And, if we do not, we have only ourselves to blame.

These five women have struggled for a life they believed would be worthwhile. Their stories show how social relations in white North American society have co-constituted women's relentless pursuit of thinness.

CHAPTER ONE

PARADISE LOST

THIS IS A STORY of romance, except that here the heroine does not overcome the hardship — the separation from her fiancé — in a manner that ensures the happy ending. Instead, the heroine has turned "fat and ugly," by her own description, and lost all hope for recapturing paradise.

Katrina, now in her late twenties, lived most of her life in Southern Europe and South America. She described the country where her family lived in South America as her "real home" and "paradise," although when I interviewed her, she had been living in Canada for about three years.

The first theme that struck me about Katrina's life story was her description of her life in South America as "paradise." Beaches, sunshine and breeze; youth, romance and wealth, passionate love, marriage and children, and eternal happiness for ever after. She felt happy there, she had no major worries; she gave little thought to her future, except for thoughts about the man she was going to marry. Katrina had many friends; she was popular and considered herself quite attractive. The family was doing very well financially. They had a maid, who cooked and cleaned and served the meals. Her fiancé, his family and her friends were central to Katrina's life. Her days were cheerful, filled with fun, going to the beaches, movies and discotheques after school. When she was not with her friends or her fiancé, Katrina liked to watch television, mostly American shows, including soap operas. She was familiar with North American popular music, and also with North American culture in general, including popular, fashion and women's magazines.

These magazines, propagating a highly idealized version of life, can be found in all Western, developing and, to a much lesser extent, socialist countries. In the developing countries, women of relative wealth internalize the images of and desires for the life-style and the standard of contemporary feminine appearance as these are depicted in the "have" countries. Reading Western European and North American magazines and watching television programing from these countries, Katrina, along with other wealthier women in the developing world, learned to be fashion, fitness and health conscious according to North American and Western European bourgeois prescription.

Katrina's father, depicted by her daughter as a "self-made man," was a successful business man who taught his daughters to work hard, implying that this is how one succeeds. The family belonged to a fashionable club, where they spent most Sundays playing tennis, swimming and eating lunch with other members of the club. Occasionally, the family went out for dinner together and then to see a show. Katrina and her mother used to get along very well. At that time, Katrina considered her mother her best friend, someone with whom she could share everything.

Although she did not want to leave her fiancé, Katrina agreed with her parents that she should attend university to further her education. Her father wanted her to study law in North America and then to get married and live in South America with her husband. She tried to please her mother as well, who wanted Katrina to look like a "little princess Diana," and to be always "dressed to a T."

When Katrina thought about the future, she fantasized about passionate love, happiness and a beautiful home with a husband

and their children. She could not name any significant conflicts and problems she had during her years in South America, and it never occurred to her that she might have to leave "paradise." But quite suddenly her parents decided to leave for Canada, and Katrina was to follow them after spending a year in finishing school in Europe.

Katrina came from a family that was well off financially. She did not have to save for her university education, and there was enough money to send her to finishing school in Europe. She was to become the "perfect lady"; all she had to do was submit herself to the rules of the school. In Europe, however, the possibility of recapturing "paradise" began to slip away; it was as if something had broken and could not be repaired. Dislocated from her familiar situation, Katrina had a "miserable time." She hated having to be away from her friends, fiancé and South America, and she resented the rigid rules of the school. They had classes on etiquette, French, horseback riding, tennis, sewing, cooking and, above all else, on how to look, walk and act like a lady. She was determined to break the rules in the hope that she could leave (or be dismissed from) the school as soon as possible. She wanted to return to her friends and fiancé.

One way to break the rules was by not conforming to the feminine prescription of eating small quantities of non-fattening food. Katrina began to spend her free time eating and going to bars. She ate anything and as much as she could possibly put away. In six months she gained thirty pounds. She felt angry toward everyone but no one in particular, and she comforted herself with huge amounts of chocolate. Utterly unhappy, now also about herself for having become "fat," she followed her parents to Canada.

After her dreams of the future were shattered when she moved from South America and gained weight, Katrina started to feel very confused; life, she said, seemed "empty," and she felt she "had nothing to fill it with." At such an impass, the future that still seemed appealing to her — albeit not realizable at the time — was the career of a model. As a model, she said, "people would still look at me; they'd notice I exist, and then I'd have something."

During the years that followed her education in finishing school, Katrina struggled to lose weight. She dieted, binged, took laxatives in large quantities and tried various diets and pills. Whenever she lost some weight, she went out more, and noticed that men wanted her. At such times, she was more pleased with herself, thought she fell in love, wanted to get married and have children.

This pattern of dieting, binging and laxative abuse has been described in terms of the tension women experience between "perfectionistic strivings" and "unfulfilled expectations" (Boskind-Lodahl 1976, 351). Dieting has been viewed as an expression of women's struggle for self-control that would bring approval from others — mostly from men. Since, however, dieting often does not achieve the sought-for result, binging offers itself as a release from the struggle of the dieter. And, when food is available, when it is comforting, when women have no other acceptable outlets for their feelings, they turn to food. But this release is only momentary. After the binge, women feel ashamed, disgusted with themselves, and worry about the weight they have gained. In an attempt to overcome their dread of fatness, the sense of loss of self-control and the fear that their lives' aspirations will slip away in direct proportion to the amount of food they have eaten, purging the food in some form becomes a necessity, as is the decision to diet again.

Katrina was caught in this cycle. Her body may not be as badly damaged as a result of her pursuit of thinness as the bodies of many other women, and she had not been diagnosed anorexic. Yet, Katrina could have been one of the women in Boskind-Lodahl's "bulimarexia" groups. Bulimarexia refers to the simultaneous existence of bulimia (excessive eating followed by some form of purging) and anorexia (loss of appetite or rejection of food).

For a brief period Katrina would have been positioned with

other bulimic women along a continuum of what Squire calls "odd eating behaviors and attitudes" (Squire 1984, 2), ranging from anorexia to normal eating (the "eating arc"; [ibid., 7]). Later, she became what Squire called a "bulimic dieter" (1984, 11) — people who binge on huge amounts of food in relatively short period of time and use binging as an "all-purpose tension releaser as well as hunger releaser" (ibid., 11). Other groups along the eating arc include chronic dieters, noncompensatory bulimics (they binge but don't purge), situational purgers and occasional dieters.

Very few women in North America today would be among the normal eaters: those who are "perfectly content with their bodies as they are, regardless of weight" (Squire 1984, 12). The normal eater's weight hardly fluctuates; she eats when she is hungry, stops when she is full and does not give much thought to food at any other times. Given that most women in our society today do not fit this description of "normal eaters," this group would be more accurately named "exceptional," rather than "normal."

Squire's characterization of women along the continuum of the eating arc closely parallels Boskind-White's and White's (1983) description of bulimarexic women, Brown's and Forgay's (1987) depiction of women at whatever weight who want to control their weight and many other accounts of women in the pursuit of thinness. Why the perfectionism? Why do women have to measure up to all kinds of impossible standards? What has been happening to women such that weight-control has become a vehicle of alleviating our self-doubt, improving our self-esteem and our way of pleasing others? What have some of the researchers said about these questions?

Anorexia nervosa, bulimia and the various other dieting groups along the eating arc reflect a very common preoccupation with thinness in North America today, particularly among white women, and not merely the desire and practice of people who are regarded as fat in the everyday sense of the term. Women along the continuum of the eating arc have been characterized by sharing "many interchangeable traits," including "high self-doubt, low self-esteem and low self-confidence" and a "passionate desire to be thin for reasons beyond health" (Squire 1984, 13). As Squire points out, these women are also "overly concerned" with other people's opinions; they want to please others; they have a "drive" to be perfect at everything, be it mothers, daughters, wives, workers and so on, and they are afraid of falling short of the standard of perfection. Finally, these women find it difficult to express their feelings, especially anger.

Although Katrina is not Western European or North American born and raised, in terms of her family background, she fits the classical clinical description of the woman with an eating disorder. According to this description, most women who develop such disorders come from families that are economically well off. It was already noted in 1880 that anorexia nervosa was more frequent in "the wealthier classes of society than among those who have to procure their bread by daily labour" (Fenwick 1880, 107, cited in Garner & Garfinkel 1980, 647).

The predominance of the upper-middle and upper classes among women with eating disorders has been reported repeatedly in the past twenty years (Bruch 1973; Crisp, Palmer & Kalucy 1976). Case studies, biographies and autobiographies are also based on the lives of women from these classes. Binswanger's (1958) famous "Case of Ellen West," Boone O'Neill's (1982) *Starving for Attention*, Liu's (1978) *Solitaire* and Kiernan's (1983) *Jane Fonda: Heroine for Our Time* are but a few of the examples.

Shortly after Kiernan's biography of Jane Fonda was published, Fonda publicly revealed her long struggle with bulimia in an interview in *Cosmopolitan* (Janos 1985). Her example, along with recent media coverage of singer Karen Carpenter's death, headlines about First Lady Nancy Reagan and Princess Diana of Wales possibly suffering from anorexia nervosa, suggests a glamourization of women with eating disorders (Garner 1983a). Perversely, the deadly practices of the relentless pursuit of thinness have been presented as desirable by associating the pursuit with rich and/or famous women.

Although it is difficult to determine the prevalence of women who regularly binge and purge (these behaviours usually take place in secret; bulimic women are often not emaciated; and these women often do not report anything unusual about their eating patterns even when they seek professional help), the statistics we have at this point are truly alarming. In the United States, researchers found that over 10 percent of 300 suburban women shoppers who responded to a questionnaire reported a history of bulimia (Pope, Hudson & Yurgelun-Todd 1984). Surveys among college populations yielded even higher figures, ranging from 13 percent (Halmi, Falk & Schwartz 1981) to 19.6 percent (Pope et al. 1984). According to Pope and Hudson, bulimia has begun to come out of the closet in the 1980s. They estimate that, in the United States alone, one to three million women binge and purge at least once a week. Pope and Hudson note that "... we may be seeing nothing less than a national, if not international epidemic" (Pope & Hudson 1984, 38).

All researchers have found that an overwhelming majority of people with eating disorders are women. It was mostly women (60 out of 62 individuals) who responded to a Cornell University newspaper ad announcing a new psychotherapy group for students who are "food bingers" (Boskind-White & White 1983, 17). Why should this be the case? Why would it be overwhelmingly women who binge and purge and starve themselves? Who are these women? Why do we see this phenomenon now?

Many writers have tried to answer these questions, and few feel that they have definite answers to offer. Some writers continue to insist on a single-factor explanation, be it an individual woman's particular psychological make-up or an underlying biochemical imbalance that causes the psychopathology of eating disorders. A relatively early and popular view was that persons with eating disorders, particularly with anorexia nervosa, reject the traditional female roles, and excessive dieting is an attempt to negate their sexuality (Szyrynski 1973). In the psychoanalytic literature, the anorexic woman's refusal to eat has been interpreted as a "fear of oral impregnation" (Szyrynski 1973, 498) and the cessation of menstruation has been taken to support the notion that anorexics reject their femininity (Thoma 1967). Although women's sexuality is an important dimension of the relentless pursuit of thinness, the relationship between sexuality and thinness is not only mediated symbolically (as in the fear of oral impregnation). The link may be more direct as well as more complex.

In recent years, researchers have suggested that several factors interact in predisposing, precipitating and perpetuating this illness (Garfinkel & Garner 1982). They discuss the genesis and development of anorexia nervosa and bulimia in terms of the interaction of individual psychobiological, familial and socio-cultural factors. While this model is a great improvement over single-factor explanations, it is weak in explaining individual psychological development consistently in social terms. Psychology, biology, family and culture are treated as if they were all separate factors, rather than always interrelated with one another. One further problem with both the single-factor and the multidimensional models of eating disorders is the assumption that anorexia nervosa and bulimia constitute disease entities that are radically different from most women's practices and preoccupation concerning their weight. The practices of women who are not diagnosed anorexic or bulimic are viewed — by definition — as if these were healthy or normal practices (Brown & Forgay 1987).

When Pope and Hudson (1985) raise the question, why should bulimia be more common among women than men, they also suggest that, "The preponderance of bulimia in women *may* be due to social factors" (our society's demand that women be thin), or "... it *may* be due to environmental factors" (e.g., women are more involved with preparing food), or it may be due to psychological or biological factors (p. 39). These authors, however, go on to say that bulimia is more likely to be caused by a *larger underlying psychiatric disorder*, namely, by a major affective disorder: manic-depressive illness or major depression (p. 39). The major affective disorders are believed to be hereditary/biological because clinicians find most patients greatly improved after only a few weeks of pharmacological treatment (p. 89).

Although there may well be biological or biochemical abnormalities among patients in the research samples used by Pope and Hudson, it is both unnecessary and unscientific to leap to the conclusion that these abnormalities *cause* an eating disorder. Our knowledge of the relationship between biochemical processes and human behaviour is presently inadequate. The studies that are cited in support of arguments of causality are all correlational studies. Correlations only tell us that there is a mutual relationship between two events, not that one event causes another. The cause may be something entirely different than either of the two events.

To reduce the explanation of bulimia or anorexia nervosa to a single factor, such as an underlying psychopathology caused by chemical imbalance, is both misleading and dangerous. Once this explanation is offered, the inclination is to stop looking elsewhere, specifically, to stop asking: What is going on in women's lives such that we see more and more women pursuing thinness, damaging their bodies and many — inadvertantly — killing themselves? Why is this phenomenon happening now? Why here? Why to women? Why — mostly — to white women? What does the pursuit of thinness tell us about the world in which women live?

There is overwhelming evidence to suggest that sociocultural factors are somehow involved in the dramatic increase in the incidence and prevalence of the relentless pursuit of thinness (Garner & Garfinkel 1980; Schwartz, Thompson & Johnson 1982). This is not just a possibility as Pope and Hudson say. The gender, age, social class and racial distribution of eating disorders should be seen as openings toward further inquiry into the actual life situations of anorexic and bulimic patients. In glaring contrast to Western statistics, the eating disorders have been rare among populations "where there is a genuine shortage of food" (Berkow 1982, 1904). Psychiatrists in Malaysia have found anorexia nervosa to be a condition hardly known among Malaysian-born and raised peoples (Buhrich 1981). Anorexia nervosa and bulimia are also practically unknown in socialist countries (Székely 1986). These observations have suggested that anorexia nervosa and bulimia are "culturally syntonic disorders" (Garner 1983c) — they chime with the sociocultural environment of our time.

What started as a fashion and beauty ideal, serving the interests of various industries, moulding our taste in style and gaining support from the popular media has come to be called a "disease." Bulimia and anorexia nervosa are diseases of the same kind that obesity often is: they have been constructed as diseases that reflect moral, sociocultural judgements. They reflect the fear and horror of fat in our weight-conscious society. They have been produced not unlike goods are produced in a market economy. Lately, with advances in cosmetic surgery, we have witnessed the emergence of yet another "new disease," what Holub calls the "violin deformity," "which in one form or another, afflicts perhaps 75% of all women." Holub describes this deformity as follows:

> What we are talking about is when your hip pad sticks just below the rib cage, then you get narrower at the midhip, then your saddlebag swells out again in a big fat lump. (Holub 1987, C1)

Why is this called a deformity? Because this "double bulge is not considered esthetically pleasing in Western culture," we are told. It is further explained that women's lower bodies "are supposed to make a smooth, round, unbroken curve from waist to knee" (ibid.). But the lower bodies of 75 percent of women do not form this smooth, round unbroken curve! Why is it a deformity, then, rather than the norm? Equally, 75 percent of women feel that they are too fat. Why isn't, then, "feeling too fat" called a norm for women on this continent, rather than a disease?

A founding member of the Bulimia and Anorexia Nervosa Association of Windsor, Ontario, had this to say on the subject:

> Look at beauty contest winners and models over the last two decades and you'll see they're getting taller, stronger and more muscular. They are fitter, but they are also slimmer and trimmer. Those women have become our ideals, our role models. The fitness craze has pushed women to want to reach unrealistic goals. (*The Toronto Star* 8 Sept. 1983)

More and more psychologists appear to concur with this view. Yale psychologist Judith Rodin, for example, discusses the stigma attached to obesity, the positive valuation of thinness and dieting as a socially acceptable form of competition for women among the salient aspects of the development of eating disorders (Bales 1984). In addition to these aspects, writers often mention our society's view of women in general, the glorification of youth and the pressure women experience to achieve in a wider range of activities than before (Chernin 1981; Coward 1985). David Garner (1983b) has noted that the "glorification of slenderness in our society promoted by fashion merchandisers and the diet industry has persistently relayed the message that weight control reflects self-control and will lead to beauty and success."

Valuing slimness represents a relatively recent shift in beauty ideal in Western societies. As recently as 1970, Elizabeth Taylor was deemed to have the most desirable shape, but by 1976 Twiggy,the British fashion model,had the figure seen as most desirable by visitors of a wax museum (Garfinkel 1981). Now E.T. is promoting her diet book! In many societies, however, plumpness in women is still considered highly desirable, and obesity is associated with status, wealth and fertility. Within North America itself, it seems less acceptable for wealthier women to be plump than for poorer women.

One view of women's obsession with weight has been that it is an attempt to develop a body that is more similar to men's bodies. Based on a survey of 33,000 women in the United States, where 75 percent of the respondents thought that they were too fat, Susan Wooley concluded that "This striving for thinness is striving to have a more masculine-type body .... Thinness has become the cultural symbol of competency" (Sternhell 1985, 68). Wooley may be right. Competence — as defined by white bourgeois men in capitalist societies today — is a necessary requirement to enter "men's worlds," and having a body that is more similar-looking to men's may announce us as competent.

In other situations, or possibly even in the same situation, however, thinness may be an expression of women's striving for today's feminine ideal. A study of the drawings and of the comments ten anorexic and bulimic women made about their depicted ideal bodies suggests that wanting to be attractive to men was on the top of the list of their priorities (Szekely & Morris 1986).

In yet other situations the thin and masculine-looking figure may be an embodiment of vulnerability — the vulnerability of an adolescent girl or boy. I mention the vulnerability of an adolescent boy as well because free adult men in ancient Greece had as their homosexual partners young boys, who could not challenge the authority of adult males (Foucault 1985). This relationship of adult males to adolescent (looking) girls or boys points to the inequality of power relationships, which is a major constituent of the phenomenon of the relentless pursuit of thinness.

There are severe sanctions in our society against women being big, powerful and taking up space (Brown 1985). Big women are isolated, invalidated in their sexuality or treated as overly sexual and sensual. Of course, different standards are applied to what constitutes a big or fat body for a woman than for a man. Women in North America are considered fat when they are fifteen to twenty pounds over the weight suggested by life-insurance charts, whereas men may weigh thirty-five or more pounds more than these charts indicate before they are pronounced fat (Chernin 1981). It is not surprising, then, that 95 percent of all people enrolled in weight-reduction programs are women. Yet recent research suggests that it may be much more of a health hazard for men than for women to be fat. As Cheryl Lean has pointed out, there is very little evidence to support the claim that fatness causes poor health among women (*Ideas* 1987, 8). Studies of high blood pressure and coronary disease among overweight people used mostly men as their subjects. When women were used, they were found through weight-reduction groups, and it is well established that dieting itself is a health hazard, which confounds the research findings. The results of recent studies have suggested that women may in fact live longer and be generally healthier if they weigh ten to fifteen per cent *above* the life-insurance figures *and* they refrain from dieting (Squire 1984).

All the pressure on women in our society to be thinner runs counter to actual weight trends. Women's average weight (as well as height) has increased since the late 1950s. Women in the 17-24 years age group, for example, became 5-6 pounds heavier between 1959 and 1979 (Garner et al. 1980). Simultaneously, the weight of the ideal female, as presented to the public by *Playboy* centrefolds, decreased. During the same period, the average weight of women who participated in Miss America Pageants also declined, and since 1970 the winners have weighed significantly less than the contestants who did not win. Finally, between 1959 and 1979, diet article citations in the six most popular women's magazines increased by over 70 percent. According to Garner and his colleagues, these findings suggest that there has indeed been a marked shift in our society's preference toward a thinner female body ideal, and this change is likely to be related to the increased prevalence of anorexia nervosa.

In an attempt to demonstrate that sociocultural pressures to be thinner are also related to the changing roles of women toward becoming more competitive, Garner and Garfinkel (1980) studied dance and modelling students. They found that the prevalence of anorexia nervosa and excessive dieting was higher among these groups than among normal weight-control subjects of similar age and social class. Further, the more competitive the setting was for the dance students, the higher was the prevalence rate. These findings seem to support the authors' hypothesis that the risk of anorexia nervosa increases when their vocational aspirations cause individuals to focus their attention on body shape.

While it may be argued that dancers have been relatively thin prior to the beginning of the Twiggy era, the ideal for the current generation of dancers has become thinner than it was in previous decades (Vincent 1981). These dancers may weigh twenty or more pounds less than their predecessors, not because they want to be reed-thin, but because they know that the artistic directors of the ballet companies want them that way. As one director said, "I don't like to see a ballet dancer with fat legs, ... it's not very elegant to see a heavy girl jiggling around on stage" (*The Gazette* [Montreal] 18 Sept. 1987, A-6). It is not uncommon for an aspiring ballet dancer to drop 35 pounds at age 15 and weigh in at just 85 pounds at a height of 5'4". As one woman told Kathryn Greenaway, the reporter of this article in *The Gazette*, at ballet school sometimes they were weighed every other day. This woman noted that they all would "diet like crazy," and she became "obsessed with weight after having to face the scale so often" (ibid.). Under such pressure, bulimia became a favorite form of dieting for dancers.

Let us return to Katrina's story. How does the literature shed light on her life and, specifically, on what happened to her in and since finishing school? There are many conflicting explanations of the eating disorders contained in the literature. I take the conflicts and contradictions among the explanations as an invitation to explore in more depth what actually happens in women's day-to-day situations, without predefining women's practices in the relentless pursuit of thinness as psychopathology.

It seems that as a wealthier white woman, Katrina has been

particularly under pressure to attain the current ideal of attractive feminine appearance. She was well instructed in many of the lessons on femininity prior to her arrival at finishing school. She knew women had to be attractive to men. She knew that she was also expected to obtain a university degree and have a career of her own. But femininity, as it was defined for her, was to be the number one priority in her life. That's what she was going to learn more about in finishing school. She was to polish her skills in ladylike manners and behaviour. Katrina did not go along with all of the instructions, however. She did not "watch her figure." She ate when she wanted, what she wanted, and perhaps even more than she wanted.

With these acts, Katrina rebelled against the loss of "paradise" that was brought about, in part, by her parents' decision to leave South America. The idyll Katrina had enjoyed was disturbed and was coming apart at the seams. Even the fantasy of eternal happiness could not be maintained in her new surroundings. In the new setting, Katrina began to see some of the artificialities of the life for which she was to be prepared, and said "no" to it. She decided — at some level of awareness — that she did not want and, perhaps, could not afford any longer the life-style that was held out for her as the ideal. Eating was her way of saying "no."

The literature we have looked at so far says nothing about women eating as an act of rebellion. Feminist writers, however, have begun to suggest that this may well be the explanation: women turn to food because they don't have access to power. Katina Noble argues that anger is at the heart of women's compulsive relationship to food (*Ideas* 1987). Since women are not allowed to express their anger at being powerless, they almost literally "eat it down" (p. 12). Women internalize and bottle up anger and swallow it down with food. Important, though, as the relationship between dieting and binging is (as the examples of dancers demonstrate), it is not the only thing that leads women to eat large amounts of food. Women eat because they have access to food, because it makes them "feel good," as Judith (another interviewed woman) said, and because of the lack of things in their lives which make them feel better.

This relationship with food, however, also makes many women's lives painful. As she lost her slim figure, Katrina felt less and less attractive to men. She did not want to see any men or date anyone, and she grew quite miserable. She wanted to hide, and hid behind piles of food. Suddenly, she said, she realized that she had "nothing to live for." She cried about having no goals, no sense of purpose or direction in life. With the "loss" of her slim figure, her future became unsettlingly indeterminate, and there was little in her experience to prepare her for such a situation.

There is nothing personal about Katrina's images of her body, although advertisers and medical experts tell us that body image is "deeply personal" (Holub 1987, C2). Some go as far as saying that already at a very young age we have an "intrinsic" sense of whether our shapes are going to "work for" us or not (ibid.)! I find such statements mystifying and dangerous. There is no evidence that an intrinsic sense of shape exists at all. All evidence points in the direction that our sense of our bodies *develops* in the processes of *learning*, and these are *social* processes, not psychobiological ones given at birth, that somehow unfold without social-interpersonal mediation.

Those so-called experts who speak of an intrinsic sense of shape would be well advised to take note of events such as beauty pageants for pre-schoolers that feature a swimsuit competition (*The Globe and Mail* 6 Jan. 1986). Three- to five-year-old children do not parade down aisles in little bathing suits unless someone puts them there and tells them what to do. They do not discover on their own by age six or even earlier that their thighs are too fat and think they should stop eating ice cream and other fattening foods. As Simone's story will clearly demonstrate, girls are pressured from the time they are small children to be slim and pretty.

Besides feeling "fat and piggish," Katrina began to find "all sorts of faults" with herself. She came to dislike her nose, her thighs and legs. She wanted to look "slim and pretty" again, because when she was slim and pretty she was happy. For Katrina, the thin and pretty body held the promise of the fulfilment of the fantasy of "romantic love" and "eternal happiness forever after."

Women worry about their appearance; they come to despise their bodies; they diet, have their noses "fixed," their breasts enlarged or made smaller, the fat suctioned out of their thighs or simply work to "develop nicer legs" (Corner 1988a, C21) because they know that what their bodies look like really matters. They know that they have to have a certain kind of appearance to be deemed attractive, to have dates, to find better jobs, to keep those jobs and be promoted in them. Women of colour and Black women in North America know that no matter how much they try to "improve" their bodies, they can never be *the image* that is required for many jobs. Black women may have tried to straighten their hair to *pass* for jobs usually given to white women. They can be slim and sleek; they can smile; they can reflect men; they can be competent in their jobs; but they can't be white. By undergoing cosmetic surgeries, Michael Jackson and, apparently, Diana Ross have tried to look more "white" — that is, successful; in a racist society the image of the attractive woman is white.

Concerns with her body occupied Katrina despite her being involved in full-time studies and part-time work. Work and study were important to her, but not more so than her appearance. Perhaps these concerns became even more important to Katrina after she came to Canada. It was then that she really "lost paradise." It was then that her parents divorced and Katrina — as most children do after their parents' divorce — stayed with her mother. They had less money; she also had to work. As a worker, like her mother, she was far from well paid. It was too late for her to really consider such a career. As a single woman, she could have barely survived financially on her own. Katrina, like most other women alone, would have had to depend on a man's wages. Achieving the life-style that was presented to her as the ideal lay outside the realm of possibilities unless she was able to attract a man of relative wealth. This, however, required that she become fashionably thin.

Katrina, like many other women in North America, wanted both to fulfil women's traditional roles and excel academically. Boskind-Lodahl (1976) found that women with eating disorders sought to be very much like their mothers, because being mothers and wives was socially approved and accepted. These women, however, also wanted to live out the academic goals and professional aspirations their mothers had abandoned in favour of raising a family. The women (the daughters in Boskind-Lodahl's group) did not perceive academic achievement as rewarding in and of itself. Boskind-Lodahl observed that "…continued success in academe was essential to feelings of self-worth, but the pressure to achieve, with its rewards, was expected to be forgotten and tucked away in exchange for the fulfilment that marriage and childbearing could bring" (p. 348). This is how it was for Katrina as well.

To examine further the questions, why women, why mostly white women, why in the "have countries" are we pursuing thinness, and why now, we need to look in more detail at the "dos" and "do nots" in women's lives. With what rules of behaviour have women been raised? What has Katrina learned?

First, the imperative of being ladylike. At finishing school she was taught the "proper way" to act, talk, and look like a lady. Proper ladylike manners include knowledge of etiquette, French, horseback riding and playing tennis, as well as the skills of entertaining and conversing with men. A proper lady, Katrina learned, should always be fashionable, yet dress in a simple style. Furthermore, she should know how to flirt.

Katrina first learned the importance of having a "good time," enjoying herself with her friends. "Fun" was defined as spending a lot of time with her peers, swimming, riding, going to shows and discos. Picnics, family gatherings and outings, strolls along the beaches were further ways to enjoy oneself. Going out to good restaurants, trying different gourmet foods is also "fun." One need not have any thoughts about tomorrow; it will be much like today, only perhaps even better: little work, lots of play, warm weather and sunshine. Finally, being passionately in love makes the present even more like paradise.

Yet, from time to time, Katrina felt that having a husband and children was "not enough." She thought that there should be something else in her life beside a family; something she was interested in, some work of her own.

The line of work that attracted Katrina and engaged her imagination more than any other was that of being a model. Models are noticed and looked at, she said. By being looked at and admired, they exist. Katrina, however, has not worked as a model; she thought she was too short and not thin enough, and it was "too late" for such a career. The point remains that the work she longed to do was work that required treating her body as an object for others. Through being an object for others' consumption, the body — herself — would have become worthy of men's attention.

It was also impressed on Katrina that she should strive to be "successful." She learned that she could achieve success by being ladylike, by men finding her attractive, by being "the best looking," and by working very hard, both at her appearance and her studies. Doing well in her studies is important, because she should attend university and earn a degree in some "respectable" profession, such as law. Being successful means being a "winner." The lazy become "losers." Being successful also means being powerful. A woman may become powerful (successful) and belong to the group of the prestigious (to society's élite) if she is well-liked by men.

Girls and women should, above all else, be pretty. They have to dress well at all times and look like a "little Princess Diana" always "dressed to a T," as Katrina's mother said. They should not, however, wear flashy clothing; dress should be simple, functional and in good taste.

Katrina learned that a woman must take care to be and remain slim so men will be attracted to her. She should not eat beyond the point of satisfying her hunger. She should exercise regularly to keep in shape. Women should work hard to be "number one" in terms of their appearance. It is very painful and leaves a scar for life, if a woman cannot be "the best looking" or at least considered among the best looking.

The most terrible thing for a woman is to look "fat and piggish," in Katrina's words. She will feel appalled by her own appearance, and men will want to have nothing to do with her. Everything about her will be "off." She will not be able to dress attractively; she will be restrained in terms of how much of her body she can allow others to see. Her thighs will become too big, her legs too fat, her face too round.

A woman should be bright and well informed: she should be able to carry on conversations with men about any topic, including local and world politics. She also needs to be bright in order to earn a university degree. She should be brighter than all other women she knows — "number one" among all the bright women.

She should also be a "good daughter." Being a good daughter means living by the rules and regulations of one's parents, doing exactly what they want her to do. She eats the food offered to her, lets nothing go to waste, for instance. She studies at the school of her parents' choice and pursues the field or career they deem best for her. She wears what, according to her mother, is in "good taste."

A good daughter works hard, she helps with housework (if there is any to be done). She is meticulous, well organized and punctual. She tries very hard not to disappoint her parents and to deserve what they give her, especially the money they spend on her. She sets herself high goals with regard to the man she aspires to marry. He has to be outstanding in every respect, wealthy or potentially wealthy, excellent company and a good father in the future.

Katrina believed that a woman's most important vocation in life is to be married and raise children. She should be most concerned with how to attract "the man of her life" and how to please and keep him. She should also be passionately and romantically in love with the man whose wife she will be. She should strive to have a nice and comfortable house, in which they will live happily ever after.

These are some of the values, norms, ideals and aspirations that Katrina internalized. We don't know what she would have been like, what she would have learned, if she was raised in a society where women were not valued primarily for their ability to present themselves as attractively feminine and as apparently perfect in all regards. We don't know what would have happened if it did not matter what the exact shape and size of a woman's body was and if it mattered a whole lot more what a woman knew and how she felt about what was happening in her life and in the world in general.

We don't know what would have happened if Katrina's and other women's mothers could have had work of their own, meaningful work; if they were not talked to and treated in every way differently than boys from birth only because they were girls. Would we see the relentless pursuit of thinness here and now if women were not always taught to "reflect men" (Cline & Spender)? If women could learn to acknowledge and develop needs of their own, rather than serving and catering to men?

The values, norms of behaviour, images, ideals and aspirations Katrina has learned and tried to live by are similar to those that feminist therapists and researchers have described for all women. They are certainly similar to what Liz, another women whose story is presented in this book, sought to actualize.

Katrina's life situation, however, also differed from Liz's in significant ways. Through wealth, Katrina learned about enjoying the present, introducing a life-style and certain aspirations that were unavailable to Liz. Furthermore, there are a number of similarities in the descriptions of values, norms, ideals and expectations — as we shall see — that are more apparent than real. For instance, the meaning of being ladylike is not identical for Liz and Katrina, although they both spoke about the necessity of looking and acting like a lady. Katrina, by virtue of her parents' social and economic position, was expected at all times to act as a lady and to complete a one year program (full-time, residential) in a prestigious finishing school in Europe. Liz, on the other hand, was not sent by her parents to enrol in a finishing course; she did this "on her own," because she was interested in the course and thought she would acquire knowledge that would enhance her work options. There is clearly a difference between these two situations that is tied to the women's socio-economic location.

Although both Liz and Katrina spoke about wanting to be married and to have a family, Katrina's vision of marriage and family appears much more romantic than Liz's. Implied in the view of marriage Katrina holds is the availability of substantial material means freeing the woman from financial concerns. This difference also points to the fact that Katrina came from a much wealthier family than Liz. As a child, Liz saw her mother worry about how she would pay the mortgage, feed the family and buy new clothes at least for Liz's father, while Katrina knew of no such concerns. The life stories in this book provide some of the context necessary to understand that even though the words the women used and the goals that can be discerned may be quite similar, the sense of the words varies greatly depending on their life situations. The words we learn ignore class, racial and other differences, but when we listen carefully to people's life stories we begin to understand that sex/gender is not the sole constituent of our difference.

The fantasy of becoming a princess and living a life of wealth, comfort and happiness can be nurtured in a context in which girls learn little about women's actual conditions and realistic possibilities in most countries in the world. The lack of accurate information about women's situations in Canada and elsewhere can be attributed, at least in part, to the media's portrayal of women's lives. Researchers of the Canadian Advisory Council on the Status of Women found that 15- to 19-year-old girls had a vision of their future lives that hardly resembled women's actual conditions in this country (Baker 1985). The girls thought that they could move easily from school through any career to marriage and raising children. Three-quarters of them expected to attend university, and more than half of those who wanted to be employed believed that they would have professional or managerial jobs. The girls depicted marriage in highly romantic terms and imagined that their husbands would be professional men, especially doctors and lawyers. The finding that adolescent girls held unrealistic and traditional aspirations came as a surprise to the Advisory Council's researchers.

If we look at the instructions girls receive in this country, these findings are hardly surprising. Even though some girls may come to the realization during their teens that they, too, could be lawyers, doctors or other professionals, none of these newly opened up possibilities have eradicated the importance of attractive appearance. The girls who compete for the "Miss Teen Canada" title are a sad reminder that first and foremost they want recognition for their attractive appearance.

As Dyer (1982) has commented, in our society "Women become the imagined fetishes of men — passive, narcissistic, exhibitionist ..." (p. 92). Advertising experts have long viewed women as "natural narcissists" who see everything and everyone as relating to them personally (Fishburn 1982, 163). When women are charged with being narcissistic, it is often forgotten that it is because they are taught to be this way that they learn to constantly watch over every spot on the surface of their bodies. Women learn to see themselves through the eyes of others. In advertisements, women are portrayed looking worried over a wrinkle around the mouth, an unwanted hair, hair that is too thin or lacking body or a pimple on the face. Conversely, women are also depicted admiring themselves; they "stare out blankly in a stupor of self-adoration. And there is something about the stupidity and vulnerability of some of these poses that invites humiliation" (Nunes & White 1973, 52).

Ads, popular books, television programs, movies, the daily newspapers and even the school curricula have been instrumental in fostering women's preoccupation with their appearance in general and, more recently, with their weight in particular. These materials do more than merely mirror our conditions and their meanings; they "teach us ways of thinking and feeling, generally through fantasy and dreaming" (Dyer 1982, 72).

It is in this way that girls as young as twelve or thirteen years of age already know that "Girls are supposed to care about their looks a lot. Be graceful, sensitive, very sensitive .... Girls are not supposed to be put in jail, drink, wrestle or be fat" (Larrick & Merriam 1973, 22). These girls in a New York State school also knew that they were supposed to be "vain," to "have class, love diamonds and minks and stuff like that," that they were supposed to be obedient servants to men (p. 22).

The girls Nancy Larrick and Eve Merriam (1973) talked to also knew that because they were "affected" by their menstrual cycles they could not be presidents. Women learn early in life that they do not know how to do things; "doing" is not their job. Advertising specialists have been in the business of making sure that men act, women appear. The caption of a cartoon portraying a little boy assembling an airplane as a little girl hands over to him a broken toy for repair reads as follows: "Boys fix things; Girls need things fixed" (Darrow 1970). Is it any surprise, then, that by the time girls reach first grade they know that their job is to be pretty?

A six-year-old girl, when asked, "What do you want to be when you grow up," answered, "a princess.... because a princess is pretty and nice" (Nunes & White 1973, 46). Susan Brownmiller (1984) wrote that "The fairy princess remains one of the most powerful symbols of femininity the Western world has ever devised, and falling short of her role model women are all feminine failures to some degree" (p. 67). Many of these "feminine failures" are today's anorexic and bulimic women.

Of course, one can't be a princess without a prince. In learning to conform to all the rules of femininity, women are "trained to need men, not sexually but metaphysically," wrote Dworkin (1983, 81). She went on to say that

> ... women are brought up to be the void that needs filling, the absence that needs presence. Women are brought up to fear men and to know that they must please men and to understand that they cannot survive without the help of men richer and stronger than they can be themselves, on their own. (p. 81)

It is not by "nature" that women are "the void that needs filling," "the absence," or the "Other" (de Beauvoir 1961). They become absent through the class society that organizes social relations around the means of production and gender differences in each of the classes. Certain men in class society are also "the absence," only they fill the void more often by alcohol than by food. Men, however, are not trained systematically to need and serve women, as women are trained to need and serve men. Men, by and large, have learned to protect themselves from bodily abuse. They are economically privileged and less likely to depend on women financially. Lately, men of higher income have been learning that they do not have to support women financially at all (Ehrenreich 1984); they can pick them up and discard them as one may do with toys, free of guilt and other consequences. Women's training, however, has not caught up with this new development. They may keep preparing and waiting for the prince, who will never come.

Before she went to finishing school in Europe, Katrina thought of herself as "slim and pretty". Although she was not completely satisfied with everything about herself, she liked what she saw when she looked in the mirror. Over the past three years, Katrina has been trying desperately to become "pretty again." She has been dieting, binging and purging. She had to be hospitalized a few times for dehydration and cramps due to laxative abuse.

When upset, disappointed, lonely or unloved, Katrina has turned to food.

Since her arrival in Canada, she has completed a university program and worked in various paid jobs, both for the money and to learn about what kind of work interested her. She lost some of the weight she had gained in Europe and began dating again. She felt that as she was becoming thinner men were more attracted to her. She has both welcomed their attention and found herself in conflict over which one she was truly "in love with." This latter question is particularly important to her in light of her desire to get married in the near future and to have children.

To this day Katrina is upset that her picture was not included in the high school yearbook among those considered "the best looking."

CHAPTER TWO

THE AGONY
OF SLENDERNESS

SIMONE SPENT MUCH of her time alone as a small child watching television, drawing and, later on, reading. Sometimes she sat in the kitchen, watching her mother and trying to help her. She had very few friends; there did not seem to be children her age in the neighbourhood. When Simone was five years old, a relative came to visit with the family for a summer. The woman ate copious amounts of food, and Simone, trying to keep up with her in eating, gained a lot of weight that summer. By the time Simone started school, she was heavier than most of her classmates. And she was teased by others for the way she looked:

> They'd get downright mean. Just because I was fat.... I used to get dragged to the doctor and be humiliated. They'd say to Mom, "Do something with her, look how fat she is." He [the physician] would say not to ever come back unless I lost 15 pounds.

Simone's parents used to yell at her: "You're too fat, go on a diet! You look disgusting! Stop eating so much, you're becoming like an elephant!" Her parents urged her to stop eating.

Simone's birth was an "accident"; her mother was in her early forties when she was born. She grew up in a period of relative economic affluence in this country. Her family, however, was not rich. They did not own their own house. Her father had his own small business, and her mother stayed at home to raise the children. Her brothers and sisters were much older than her and were rarely at home. Some of them had already moved away and had their own spouses and children. They had little to do with Simone when she was young.

Early in her life Simone perceived very clearly and painfully that she "just didn't belong." Everyone else in her immediate family was very slim, and she was supposed to be "sleek and slim," not "fat and grumpy," as she was. She was teased, by children and by her own family, for over a decade. There wasn't a day in her life when she didn't wish to be thinner:

> I always wanted to lose weight, it was something I was going to do. It was always the first thing on my mind. I tried lots of diets lots of times and I was able to stick to them for just a little while, but then I'd go back to eating too much again.... I just wanted to be thinner; it always bothered me. My thinking was, "I'm so unhappy; I've always been unhappy. But the reason why is because I was fat. That's all people ever teased me about. So that must be really important. And once I am not fat any more I'll be happy and everything is gonna be fine." And I always used to daydream about when I was eighteen or nineteen and I was gonna be slim. It was a daydream. It never seemed real. I was so fat. There was so much I'd have to lose to ever be slim.

At home Simone learned early that she always had to be the best and "never to settle for anything less than the best." It was important to "be a lady all the time," to dress as a lady —to wear pretty dresses, not pants. It was important to be polite, to always say "thank you," to respect her elders no matter what they said and to "play hard-to-get with guys." Her parents impressed on her that what other people, neighbours and family, thought of her mattered a great deal.

Simone knew that she was supposed to get "good marks" at school and that it was important to get what she described as a "good job, such as a lawyer or a doctor." She recalled her parents telling her that if she worked very hard and for a long time, she "could make it to the top." None of her sisters or brothers have made it to the top, nor were they expected to. But Simone, younger and raised in the 1960s, received the same messages about the necessity of having a career that middle-class girls did.

Simone and her parents never got along very well. "We never talked; they always fought," she said. She felt that no matter how hard she worked, it was never "good enough" for her parents. Once Simone received an award for "the most improved student" of the year. She remembered being "ecstatic about having received an award of excellence," which she felt she truly deserved. But when she got home, she was told: "Are you crazy? You don't deserve this!"

Lately, Simone has felt close to only one brother who is severely ill and still living at home with Simone and her parents. This brother is the only person in the family who seemed to accept her for who she was, regardless of how much she weighed.

Throughout her childhood and teens, Simone daydreamed about being slim. In daydreams, as Frigga Haug (1987) noted, women are powerful and independent; they are in the driver's seat. In actuality, daydreams tell us about the limits of what women can hope for at the very most, not what objectively may be best for women. When Simone daydreamed, she imagined that by age eighteen or nineteen she would be a slim beauty. She would be irresistible; she would not have to question or earn other people's love for her. But, as she said she learned later, "When you're fat you don't realize your limitations. You think that you can look like anybody as long as you lost weight. Perfect, you'd have a perfect body if you just stopped eating ...." She tried many diets, but nothing worked; she always gained the weight back. She was beginning to resign herself to being fat for the rest of her life. When Simone was seventeen, she weighed 190 pounds.

As an outgoing, friendly person who was a good listener, who never complained about anything and smiled at all times, Simone managed to make many friends in high school. She went out more, was invited to parties and took vacations with friends. She was pleased with her life, even though it was hard at times to keep on smiling and pretending that she was "happy with everything." Simone thought that if she could be "that happy weighing that much," she could be "ten times happier being slim."

As I was listening to Simone, I found it difficult to believe that she was indeed as happy in high school as she described. She was not supposed to have any problems of her own. She was to be there for others at all times. She was never allowed to forget that she was fat:

> I have been through a lot but it's worth not being overweight. It just is. You don't know how miserable the life of a fat person is. It is a miserable life. You are filled with all kinds of insecurities. You are feeling like you really don't fit in. And you're embarrassed to do all sorts of things because you are twice as heavy as they are. Like sports.... Even things like going out for dinner.... It's not like I ate more than anybody else, but I was fat, and here I was in the restaurant wanting to eat more ... and wondering what other people were saying. Or whether they said what they did just to be nice. But you'd never let on. You'd never show how you felt. I'd always pretend I was happy with everything, and I was really outgoing and smiling all the time, rain or shine. And it just gets to you after a while.

I was reminded of my doubts about Simone's happiness when I saw a diet-centre ad that read: "Are you overweight? Are you happy? Are you kidding?" (*The Toronto Star* 26 Nov. 1985, A17).

In the summer of grade eleven, Simone decided she was going to lose weight by not eating. She lived on lettuce leaves and black coffee — and an occasional quarter of a boiled egg when she was really hungry. After a six-week starvation diet Simone's weight fell below 140 pounds — she had lost 45 pounds — and she was told over and over again that she looked "sensational." She was, for the first time, asked out on dates. She thought, "If people think I look great now, can you imagine what they'd say if I lost 30 more pounds!"

"It felt good not to eat and lose weight. It was worth every second," Simone remembered. Family and friends praised her and commented on how great she was starting to look. She was getting asked out by men she had known before. She believed that all this was happening because she was getting thinner. It was.

A year later, Simone decided she wanted to lose some more weight. This time she went to a weight-loss clinic, where she was put on a 490 calories-per-day diet. In thirteen weeks she was to weigh 109 pounds. After going down to and below this weight, Simone was finally, and for the first time, "really happy with the way [she] looked." She "felt thin," and that made this period "the best" for her. She was beginning to look at herself in the mirror, something she could never do before without feeling disgusted with herself. She liked what she saw when her ribs and clavicles began to show.

Instead of stopping at 110 pounds as she originally planned, Simone continued dieting until she weighed no more than 94 pounds. She felt, "If I could be that happy weighing that much, then I could be ten times happier being slim." Simone felt really happy when her weight fell below 100 pounds. "I hate to admit it," she said. "I felt thin [and] that's what made it the best."

Her battles with maintaining her weight at the level she had achieved began to reflect the pattern described below:

> Your diet gets more restrictive. No fats. No dressings. You rinse your low-fat cottage cheese. Then you turn vegetarian. No meat, fish or chicken. Not even eggs or dairy. But you carbo-load on rice, pasta, potatoes. When you binge — and you do, sometimes inhaling bags of M&M's — you exercise twice as long the next day to burn off the calories.
>
> Finally, your menstrual periods stop. But you don't mind. It's one less thing to interfere with workouts.

After all, you're an athlete now. Disciplined, healthy and fit. And you're sick. And you know it.
But you can't stop. (*The Gazette* [Montreal] 18 Sept. 1987, A-6).

Like many other women, Simone could not stop. Soon she, too, started binging and purging by vomiting, taking laxatives and diuretics. Like Katrina, she had to be hospitalized for dehydration. She did not acknowledge that she was really sick when she was hospitalized. The recognition of how serious her condition had become took several more years and many more hospitalizations.

Until recently, researchers believed that patients with anorexia nervosa either actually lost their appetite or firmly adhered to their extremely reduced calorie diets (Freedman, Kaplan & Sadock 1972). Lately, however, investigators have suggested that nearly 50 percent of those with anorexia nervosa resort periodically to binging and purging or become bulimic in later phases of their illness (Casper & Davis 1980). Whether bulimia is a relatively common end-stage of anorexia nervosa or a distinct subgroup of the latter is still a topic of debate (Garfinkel, Moldofsky & Garner 1980). After a careful examination of surveys and experimental studies on the relationship between dieting (not restricted to those diagnosed anorexic) and binging, Polivy and Herman (1985) go a step further and conclude that "... the available evidence supports the hypothesis that dieting precedes binging more strongly than it does the converse hypothesis" (Polivy & Herman 1985, 195).

This certainly seems to be the case with Simone. As an adolescent she was not even a "compulsive eater." She ate about the same quantities and types of food as her friends. As a child, while she ate more than she needed to be well nourished, she did not binge. She only began to binge after she had commenced in a weight-reduction program.

The scale, the faceless inanimate object, became a powerful mediator between Simone's sense of herself and the world around her. Against her wish, she had to gain a certain number of pounds to earn her discharge after she was first hospitalized. Weighing in, for Simone, was truly an ordeal. She wanted to go home but, simultaneously, she dreaded the prospect of getting fat again. We are inundated with images of white women on scales in North America, with happy women or sad women, depending on what the scale shows. In an article reminding readers not to quit their New Year's resolutions, we see the picture of a young, thin, blonde, white woman almost leaping off the scale in joy. The caption reads: "Aiming to lose: Happiness is resolving to lose pounds and seeing positive results. The key ... is to ensure the resolution is an 'I want to' rather than an 'I have to' kind" (*The Toronto Star* 16 Jan. 1988, B2). Simone always spoke of "wanting to lose weight," not of having to. She knew that she would be happier, more accepted or loved, if she were to lose weight. In the struggle to be thinner — happier — Simone became one of many women for whom the relationship between the body she *is* and the body she *has* becomes externalized.

Once above 110 pounds, Simone was discharged from hospital. A few months later, however, she was back, to break the cycle of binging and purging. She had started to vomit blood by then and suffered from serious electrolyte imbalances.

Simone gained and lost weight, within a twenty-five to thirty pound range, on several occasions over the next four years. There came a time when, even though the scale showed she was below 100 pounds, she felt fat. During a hospitalization, following a binge, Simone wrote in her diary:

> My stomach is sticking out far enough for people to notice and think I am a big fat pig and should go on a diet. I don't want to go on a diet but I am not sure except that I feel fat. I felt fat at 94 pounds, so how good is my judgement?

As a child, Simone was very unhappy and thought she was unhappy because she was fat — the only thing people ever teased her about. Everyone in her family was slim. She believed that fat was unattractive, ugly, disgusting and that women especially were supposed to look sleek, slim, tall, beautiful. Her ideals, like Katrina's, were pretty, slim girls from television shows and, later, fashion models and television stars.

Simone thought that if she could lose weight she would be "really happy and everything would be fine." A fat person's life is a "miserable life, ... filled with all kinds of insecurities. You're feeling like you really don't fit in. And you're embarrassed to do all sorts of things because you're twice as heavy," Simone explained. Her words about how she felt when she looked at herself one night leave us with little doubt about how important it was to her to be thin:

> The other night ... I looked at myself in the mirror and was horrified at what I saw. It was this big, fat, ugly slob in the reflection which could be no one but me. I threw an ashtray at it until the reflection shattered into a thousand pieces.

A woman who is not thin enough invites punishment — she may be seen as overly sexual and used and abused, Simone suggested. Listening to Simone one gets the sense that fat is not a possible way of being for a woman; it may be better for a woman to be dead than fat. Simone was hospitalized for several months at a time during the past three years, and each time her condition was very serious. In hospital, she gained weight, but she did not stop binging and purging for more than a few days. After discharge from the hospital, she would binge and purge several times daily, almost every day. For years she has lived her days thinking about little else than food and dieting; she simply had no time for anything else — as she said.

How are we to understand Simone's overwhelming preoccupation with food and dieting? This question has tortured her, and puzzled and frustrated the many professionals who have been involved with her and other women who relentlessly pursued thinness. That she has been desperate time and again is obvious, even from this brief account of her life. Simone often thought about killing herself, and at least once tried taking her life. This was the "only way out" that she could see to end her agony. The diaries she lent me speak of despair and dread page after page:

> Mom, you deserve a perfect daughter, not something like me.... Dad, you buy me extravagant presents and you call me your princess.... Princesses are beautiful to look at and they possess the utmost fineness. You were cursed with an ugly, fat and stupid female for a princess.

Simone has wanted desperately to be "someone special," preferably a "beautiful princess," although she knows this is a fantasy. Nonetheless, she continues struggling to perfect her looks, while hoping to stop binging and purging so she does not inadvertantly kill herself. Now and then, when she feels that someone cares, she is filled with a glimmer of hope, and being thin ceases to be the central issue in her life for a fleeting moment.

Simone's is certainly not an isolated story. I have talked to many other women — women hospitalized for starving themselves and women never hospitalized for starving themselves — who hate and despise themselves for what they have eaten, for what they should have eaten but did not, or for how much or how fast they ate. Many live in utter shame and despair, feeling totally isolated and helpless. They are attuned to the slightest changes in their bodies, and whatever they feel is related to those changes. There comes a time when they begin to feel nothing, then "go numb," as Simone often described herself. Feeling nothing becomes preferable to the agony of self-loathing. These women have spoken of themselves as "hollow" and "empty shells."

Awareness of the potentially lethal consequences of binging and purging has not discouraged many women, including Simone, from continuing the practice, as we see from her diary:

> There is no doubt that if I continue as I am now I will inadvertantly kill myself. I will probably die wretching and puking my fucking brains out. The sooner the better, as far as I am concerned. I hate myself more and more every day. I can't stand looking at myself in

the mirror. I am so disgusted, I want to break the reflection every time I do.

Simone has sometimes thought that the only way to be free from the urge to binge is by death. Binging, besides satisfying her desire for food, is a process Simone described as a "release. But later all the awful feelings set in." She depicted the binge as follows:

> When I first make up my mind to do it, it is ... [satisfying], at first, when I say, "O.K., I am going to binge." And then, after the first thing I eat, whatever it is, that's when it starts: "Oh, my God! It's disgusting! Look it, you can't even stop now; it's disgusting. You're disgusting! Why would you do that? Why would you eat all that food just so that you turn around and bring it all up? What kind of a warped person are you?" And it was even worse when I was in the hospital, knowing there I was for help and I was doing it more than ever.

When I asked Simone what it was like to be fighting the urge to binge, she said:

> I don't know if I can compare it to anything else in my life.... (Pause) O.K. Maybe when you were a teenager and you really wanted to go somewhere and your mother said you could not go; the whole time you'd be thinking about what you could have been doing at your friend's house. No matter what you may be doing you're always thinking about that. That's what it's like.

It seems that after a while the binging and purging take on a life of their own, so to speak, and the person can no longer tell whether she is hungry or she is "just craving food" and wants the experience of release Simone has described. Sometimes the disgust she felt may have kept the binging and purging cycle going. Often, when Simone felt "so fat" and could not think of anything else but how fat she felt and of salvation through death she turned to food. Food is, after all, comforting and easily available. One such night Simone wrote:

> I binged tonight on a big muffin, one piece of toast with peanut butter, six crackers and four social tea biscuits. It wasn't a big binge, but a binge nonetheless. How am I going to get over this, it's so damn frustrating.... Maybe I do need some more time there [in the isolation room].
>
> I was in the drug store earlier. The urge to pick up a box of laxatives was overwhelming. I was facing the shelf, contemplating the pros and cons. Finally, I walked away from the section without picking anything up. Tonight I regret not having bought them. I can't distinguish hunger and the urges to binge.

How did food become Simone's major preoccupation, and how did it come about that being fatter than the children around her became the central issue in her life?

For those living well above the poverty level, food is available in abundant quantities and varieties. We are constantly invited to consume more, to try a new brand or the same brand with slightly different ingredients, to have another snack, to visit a new restaurant, to sample another product, without cessation. From their earliest age, children are introduced into becoming consumers, and food is a primary area of consumption. In supermarkets, we see very young children asking, begging, crying for or simply grabbing a box of the latest brand of cereal, gum, cookies or candy. These children grow up to be consumers who may never have gone hungry for long nor had to say "no" to almost any food they desired. The children become adults for whom it is perfectly natural to ask for and expect the newer, improved, better item. Our desires and needs are structured significantly by discourses and practices of advertising, for which the sources, organization and interests are largely invisible. With the best of intentions, we may perpetuate these discourses and practices by suggesting to a friend that she should consider weight lifting to build a gorgeous body, or buying certain products that will help her lose weight.

It is true that in the popular media we rarely see women eating, unless they are already reed-thin and have earned their snack, typically by workout. When we do see women eating, they are usually consuming low-calorie desserts and main courses. We certainly see women selling, buying and preparing food. Even these women are sleek, slim and white — with the few exceptions of the very few older women that are portrayed in the media. The absence of portraying adult women eating regular foods is peculiar. Taken as a whole, the images suggest either that women have already indulged in food, and they better "watch it," or that they have eaten all the wrong foods (wrong means fattening, for them but not for members of their families), and it is time that they "smarten up."

Food, for those who have learned thoroughly that it is natural to want the latest, the best and the most for their money, may become the enemy once slimness is equated with being attractive. Seeing, smelling, handling or even talking about food becomes dangerous. A city like Toronto, as Simone noted, is full of temptations. Desserts and fast foods are particularly hard to avoid. For her to fight off the invitations to try a bite, just one bite, requires an ongoing struggle. References to food and dieting exist side by side in women's magazines and elsewhere. In a recent issue of *Ladies's Home Journal* (Feb. 1988), for example, we see an ad for "Chicken: New Ideas for an Old Favorite" (p. 95), followed by a full-page picture of a woman trying (unsuccessfully) to button her jeans. The title of a feature article, "How Not to Get Fat This Winter," is written through half her body. In the same issue there is a picture of various coloured pills with the caption: "Lose weight with the help of phenylpropanolamine hydrochloride" (p. 134), followed on the next page with large pictures of meat loaves (p. 136). In case the readers fail to put these messages together, there is one ad in this journal that does it for them. Here, on a full page, we see an empty glass, with traces of an ice cream sundae. In a corner there is a picture of "Stay Trim" — a "new diet gum," with "delicious and safe to weight loss" written on the package. About two-thirds of the way down the page, in bold black letters, we can read the following: "By the time your diet pill helps you resist the temptation, it may be too late (p. 81)." Even restaurant reviews tell us that "... the baklavah baked on the premises is worth breaking a diet for"! But then, aren't diets made to be broken?

Food is a major area of concern when there is too little of it, and people starve. But it can also exclude almost anything else when there is plenty of it around. When we hear time and time again, "Try it, you deserve it," when food is tied emotionally to a sense of fulfilment, when women have deprived themselves of food by chronic dieting and when it is affordable, food can also be a preoccupation. Those who have dieted know that food is available, and they can, but must not, purchase it lest they gain weight. Since the study of men who participated in a semi-starvation experiment (Keys et al. 1950), it has been argued that dieters are also people who have starved. Many of the young men in this study started binging and purging as food was made more available to them during the refeeding period of the experiment. The preoccupation with and the anxiety over obtaining enough food persisted among the men long after the study terminated. Several of the men became chefs or worked in other food-related fields in the years following their participation in the experiment. Many anorexic women cook and bake for others, but eat none of the food themselves. Many of them are also employed in jobs that require handling and preparing food or planning menus.

The conflicts over food need to be understood in social and psychological terms, but the effects of starvation or semi-starvation on the body cannot be ignored either. People who have starved want food because they have not eaten enough, and they also desire it because it is there, everywhere, enticing them. The dieters — so many white North American women — have learned to keep consuming without even asking: Do I want this? Do I need this? Is this what I need? Consuming is not a choice; "freedom" consists, at most, of which item to purchase.

Speaking of her plan to find a clinic that would help her lose 10 pounds, Simone stated:

> I just want to lose weight. And that's more important to me than anything else.... I just want to be slim and I want to be tiny. I want to be able to wear whatever.... Wake up in the morning and say, "O.K., I want to wear this." Be able to put it on without having to worry, "Oh, my God," you know, "it's too tight." And just wear it and be comfortable that I don't look too fat.

Just as in fashion advertisements, Simone wanted to be able to wear anything, feel comfortable and look good in it. If we look closely at fashion trends, however, it's not true that models can wear anything at all. They wear clothes that suit women who are very thin, not any clothes at all. At the time of my interviews with Simone, the fashion pages of the newspapers announced "new slender shapes" (*The Globe and Mail* 17 Dec. 1985). The message was clearly spelled out:

> It is inescapable, however, that clothes are thinner, and bodies must be thin enough to accommodate them. The implications are clear: there will be no surcease from the rigors of exercise and dieting during the winter months.

The writer of this article, Bernadine Morris, went on to speak about "skinny skirts" and "slender dresses", a "clean, cool look at the neckline" and the "particularly feminine look" that clothes curving "softly around the body and into the waistline" can yield. The key words are "skinny," "slender" and "feminine" (read: skinny and slender equals feminine), not comfort in wearing any clothes on a body of any shape and size.

It's been only recently that women, bigger women with more money, have begun to demand fashionable clothes in larger sizes (*Time* 4 May 1987). The industry has responded because they recognized that there was too much money to lose if they did not cater to women size 14 and larger — nearly half of all women in the United States. They have realized that nearly half of the women in the size 16 and larger group are fashion-conscious young women with hefty disposable incomes — the industry could not afford to lose their purchases. Despite this trend toward fashion in larger sizes, most of our images of fashionable appearance continue to be of slim, slender and skinny models — the models Simone tried to emulate.

Although Simone talked about her desire to find a man to be married to, she has not actively pursued finding a husband. She has been so caught up in her binges and purges and preoccupations with dieting that other concerns, apart from the general notion of wanting to be attractive, have fallen by the wayside. She would like men on the street to turn and take a second, admiring look at her, but, she said, she also wanted to be "inconspicuous." She did not want people to know that she had "this problem," and feared that if they looked very closely they might somehow see that something was not quite all right about her, that she was a "sick woman." Simone was suggesting that it is not enough for a woman to be "fashionably thin"; she must also look like "health embodied." A woman who does not appear attractive (thin) and healthy is not wanted by men.

Simone was told repeatedly that if she worked hard and persistently she could make it to the top; she could be successful and happy. For periods when Simone persevered, she achieved in her studies and she earned a college degree. But Simone has never been convinced that she was smart enough; she never believed that she could become a professional. She has wondered for a long time what her I.Q. was; she thought she could not be worth much unless she was in the top two percent of the population. She seemed convinced that she must not be in that range, therefore, intellectual achievement was not her lot in life. Anything less than what — in everyday life — is viewed as exceptional or brilliant is not worth the effort. Being ordinary seemed unacceptable to Simone.

Simone's desire to be extraordinary should not surprise us. Nor should we see it as one manifestation of the perfectionistic tendencies of anorexic women, as so much of the literature has done. Anorexic women have been described as high achievers with low self-esteem, who train themselves to consider hunger pleasant and even desirable. Hilde Bruch wrote that bearing the hunger and seeing themselves as getting thinner gives anorexic women "so much pride that they are willing to tolerate anything" (Bruch 1979, 4).

In reality, the anorexic woman is doing nothing different than trying to live up to the images of being extraordinary that are offered to her. Her pursuit is part and parcel of the image of the "new woman" who can juggle career, home, friends, family, fashion, fitness and an exciting social life. The "new woman" is simply brilliant in all regards; she handles any and every situation like a pro and, of course, manages time well. Aware at some level of the impossibility of living up to this image, the anorexic woman focuses on one aspect — thinness — and tries to go as far as she can with it.

The problem with depicting the anorexic woman's striving as "amazing, even awe-inspiring," and focusing on her "iron determination" to achieve a "skeleton-like" appearance, as Bruch does (ibid.5), is that this description radically separates the practices of women diagnosed anorexic from numerous other women's struggles to approximate the image of superwoman. This separation hides the social roots of women's seemingly isolated, individual struggles. Bruch, like many other clinicians, fails to recognize that no one, including the women who have been diagnosed as anorexic or bulimic, lives in a vacuum. No person alone can take pride and joy in her thinness. There has to be an atmosphere and a social context in which something comes to have the possibility of being regarded as an object of pride.

Sometimes even writers who consider themselves feminist lose sight of this point. When they turn to clinical writings such as Bruch's with a view of reinterpreting their contents from a feminist perspective, they often bypass the notion of psychopathology which is taken for granted in Bruch's work. Despite Bruch's references to anorexia as a "sociocultural epidemic" (pp.

vii-viii), which is exacerbated by fashion's emphasis on thinness, and to the stigma attached to being a fat woman, Bruch's description is decontextualized and ahistorical. The reader is never led to question how and why we construct certain phenomena as normal or psychopathological.

It is only in a certain social-historical climate that trying to approximate the images of this "new woman" can become desirable. While we need to recognize that particular aspects of this new image may have emancipatory potential — for example, opportunities in work that were previously closed to women have opened up — we must also see that this new image has also meant new shackles for women. They now have to fit more molds than ever before; they now have to stand and walk competently in all kinds of new shoes; and they always have to be willing to do more — and better than ever.

Boskind-White and White (1983) situated the increasing emergence of "bulimarexia" in the late 1970s within the post-Second World War North American context. They discussed the phenomenon in relation to women's changing roles in a society dominated by the popular media and big business. They further claimed that with the rise of feminism, women have experienced conflicting values as new roles open up for them. These women, daughters of Betty Friedan's *The Feminine Mystique*, were encouraged by their fathers to achieve academically as well as professionally, but they have been particularly rewarded for "feminine" behaviour. Expressing this conflict, one of Boskind-White's clients notes, her parents wanted her "not to succeed and to succeed at the same time," leaving her stuck with the confusion of "wanting to do well, but then being afraid that it was not O.K. to do well" (p. 76).

This confusion is not unique to "bulimarexic" women. Most women experience it. We find that our efforts at being outspoken, competent in areas new to women and especially critical of authority of any kind are met with rejection, disapproval or outright punishment. We are then left with having to pick up the pieces, so to speak, and put ourselves back together. But we look for examples of this in vain in glossy magazines and even in the plain black-and-white print of newspaper articles.

Instead, we are told that we should know how to take care of ourselves, our needs. Women should know what they want and how to ask for it. Now, in an article in *The Toronto Star* Corner tells women that they must make every effort to bring "wellness" into their lifestyle: "Simply put, wellness is a belief that your level of wellbeing depends on the health of your body, mind and spirit" (1988b. G1, G5). As defined here, wellness is an *individual*, not a collective, achievement. In the words of Mary Pat Moore (a woman interviewed in Corner's article), "I came to the realization that I was the only one who had control over making me feel better about my own life. If I take good care of myself, I'm less dependent on others taking care of my needs. I can more directly get the things out of life that I want" (ibid.).

It is curious that, in all of the articles on becoming this "new" (and "well") woman, there are never any obstacles that the heroine simply cannot overcome. Everybody always succeeds. If they didn't, it would be their fault, of course. They did not try hard enough. They did not get the right kind of help or experiment with the range of techniques now available. The heroines always know (or have just discovered) what it is they want, and there is never any question about the right(eous)ness of their desires.

In the popular media, women only ever have "problems" that the "right attitude," expert advice and appropriate props can overcome. Simone, like many other women, has tried to adopt the proper attitude ("I want to," rather than "I have to," lose weight); she has tried to follow experts' advice. These so-called experts have been more than willing to rush in with their paraphernalia to help "melt away" fat. The experts can help, but cannot do it for you, seems to be the motto. They can give ingenious tips, but, ultimately, it is the woman's willpower and sensibility that will guarantee the promised results. The tips women are offered seem to be endless. *Mademoiselle*, for example, a magazine many of the interviewed women had read regularly, had a four-page feature (Nov. 1984) on "The Sinner's Diet — Twenty-Five Ways to Beat Post-Party Pudge."

In this article a cartoon-character woman, drawn with inordinately long and thin neck, skinny legs and arms and fashionably broad shoulders, tells us, among other things, to go late to a party because by then "most of the diet defeating foods will be gone." She advises women to apply dashing new lipstick and nail polish that we surely would not want to ruin with smeared food. She plays with her hair, walks around smelling perfume and clutching her breath mints one of which she may pop if she can no longer resist the smell of sweets (should there be any left). When all else fails, she might take one tiny bite of a delicacy and shove the rest in her boyfriend's mouth who, conveniently, is standing nearby! Should she go to the party alone, she is well advised to seek out a man, preferably one as far from the food table as possible, and pretend to be falling in love with him. Besides the obvious heterosexist bias here, we see that in quest of the "ideal body," other people (men — in this example) become means to an end. Relationships with others take on a wholly impersonal quality; others become objects for the body I have (or want to have). As the body of the woman who follows experts' advice becomes more and more an "it," so do other people.

This article also suggests many pre-party precautions a woman should consider taking. She could go and have her teeth cleaned — who would want to dirty those beautiful white teeth? She could do fifty jumping jacks or its equivalent to raise her basic metabolic rate and thus, presumably, suppress her appetite. Most certainly, she should be thinking about the morning after, about the terrible aftermath of the "pig out." "Burn fat, burn!" is written in one-inch letters at the top of the page. Fat is so blatantly bad, shameful and disgusting that it is the arch enemy against which a woman must always be on guard and which she must exorcise at whatever cost in labour, time and money.

In the December 1984 issue of *Glamour* magazine, there appeared a similar article entitled "152 Ways to Stay Slim Through the Fat Season" — Christmas. The article opens with a formula that can be used to calculate how much food a woman can eat (as a function of weight and activity level) without gaining weight. This is followed by a list of "temptations to think twice about" and "fifteen ways to prevent weight creep." Further headings of ingenious tips include: nine ways to work exercise into your busy day, ten calorie-burning activities, two ways to make exercise more effective, thirteen holiday survival strategies, and many more ....

The striking similarities between the practices of fitness and diet-conscious white North American women and those of the "victims of the new epidemic illness" (Bruch 1979, vii-viii) — anorexia nervosa — have not been completely ignored by these magazines. They are the very magazines that have been instrumental in fostering and maintaining the thin beauty ideal by offering endless advice to women on how to attain it. In a popular women's magazine an article appeared with the title: "When Eating — or Not Eating — Is a Sickness ...." The preamble to the article reads as follows: "Anorexia, bulimia —every weight-conscious girl [sic] should be aware of these harrowing ailments.... learn how to slim down *sanely*." The discussion on bulimia and anorexia nervosa purports to answer the question: "Is dieting dangerous?" The author concludes:

> If the current epidemic of eating disorders tells us anything, it should remind us that there are *no* safe and sure cuts to weight control, that people *can* be too thin and, finally, that if you want to be healthy and strong as well as slim, you'll have to set about it sanely, sensibly ... and *forever*. (*Cosmopolitan's Super Diets & Exercise Guide* Fall-Winter 1984, 100)

That we should control our weight is not questioned at all. The article is silent about the fact that it is dieting that leads to binging in the first place. In every instance, it is diet that sets off the intense preoccupation with food — as anorexic and bulimic patients report (Szekely & Morris 1986). According to this article, in the end, it is the woman alone who is to blame for her condition; after all, she was not "sane" and "sensible" about her dieting!

Whether one should or should not lose weight is determined by the scale and not by whether one's present weight represents a greater health risk than the risk of repeatedly losing and regaining weight would — as is the case 95 percent of the time.

I became particularly concerned about the dangers of repeated dieting when Simone mentioned that she continued to want to lose weight, this time "only about ten pounds." I was afraid that joining yet another weight-loss program might take Simone right back to where she was the first time she took part in such a program — at less than half her pre-program weight and mortally in danger. I wanted to find out how likely it was that a weight-loss clinic would take her as a client. I wanted to know what kind of screening they did, whether they were interested in the prospective client's weight history, and whether they would screen for a history of anorexia or bulimia.

Being roughly the same size (height and weight) as Simone was at the time, I decided to pass myself off as a prospective client of the particular clinic Simone was planning to contact. I dialed the clinic's number, not without considerable anxiety about what I would learn. I was worried for Simone — perhaps the clinic would take her — but I was also worried for myself. Would they take me? If they did, how would I get out of the program? Or should I stick to it, to see from the inside what it's like? And would I, could I, end up stuck with the same struggle that Simone has been fighting?

I gather that I sounded fairly anxious when I finally said that I wanted information about the weight-loss program that was advertised in *The Toronto Star*. I quickly added that I was particularly interested in learning whether they required their clients to undergo a medical examination. Without further ado it was explained to me that the program consisted of 50 percent diet and 50 percent behaviour modification. (How they figured out the percentages escapes me!) I was told that a medical and laboratory check up was required in order to establish my blood-sugar and potassium levels. If, however, I had received a recent physical and checked out in good health, this step would be skipped. At no point was I queried about how much I weighed and why I wanted to lose weight. But, I was asked how much weight I wanted to lose. When I said 10 pounds (this is how much Simone wanted to lose), I was told at length about how many calories I would be allowed to eat in the weight-loss phase and in later phases of this program. I was then offered an appointment for a free consultation. Concerning the behaviour modification component of the program, I learned only that the clinic had "expert therapists."

I kept the appointment for the free consultation. Entering the nurse's office, I was promptly told to take my shoes off and step on the scale. When the scale showed that I weighed in at the lower end of the weight range for my height and body frame, the nurse said that they could not take me. I started to explain that I do have a weight problem. I went on to present her with the story I had made up on my way over to the clinic. I said that I had gained at least five pounds over the past couple of weeks, and I was beginning to be concerned. She then questioned me about my eating habits. I threw in "lots of cakes and chocolates." I was offered the advice that I should substitute fresh fruit and yogurt for these sweets. The nurse acknowledged that, indeed, I had a problem with my eating habits, but I could not be admitted to *this* particular clinic. She explained that "We have doctors working here. They could not take the responsibility should you get ill as a result of weight loss." My wanting to lose weight was not questioned at all. The reason for sending me away was fear of malpractice suit.

Relieved, I hurried out of the room. I could not help thinking later, however, that Simone would have known how to beat the system. She would have thought of a quick method to gain weight, such as drinking plenty of water and eating salt. She also would have known what to do to temporarily increase her potassium level to avoid being detected as someone with a history of bulimia.

On my way out of the nurse's office, I noticed a sign in the waiting room. It read: "Dear Patient: Remember, the more we see you the less we see of you!" The word "patient" was a candid reminder that being fat is viewed, in this setting and elsewhere in our society, as essentially a medical condition. Doctors can be summoned to alleviate the suffering of the patient. The way in which fat is a socially constructed problem is not acknowledged inside the white walls of nurses' and doctors' offices.

Before the nurse dismissed me, she had suggested that I stay for a group session that was being held in the waiting room, so I joined a dozen or so women discussing weight and dieting. I thus had the opportunity to watch the "expert therapist" in action. I heard fat and dieting being discussed as a simple question of self-control and finding suitable substitutes for the maladaptive behaviour of compulsive eating. Behaviour was categorized as either fattening or non-fattening. A bubble bath, exercise, listening to music, taking the dog for a walk were among the recommendations made to a woman whose question was how to avoid nibbling after work. Once again, the desirability of losing weight in the first place was passed by without a comment or question.

I will never forget the moment of stepping on the nurse's scale, wondering what she'd say, wondering if I'd be trapped in the pervasive preoccupation with weight. I remembered the women I have seen stepping anxiously on other scales — in the locker rooms of swimming pools. I remembered women colleagues telling me that, after an aerobics class, they head straight toward the scale to see how much the workout was worth in terms of ounces (of water) lost. I remembered Judith, another woman I had interviewed, who worried about the "extra" pound the scale would show the following day after a snack.

It is only recently that a few authors have begun to examine more closely the question of women's wants, needs and desires. They have begun to raise these issues in the context of anorexic women's struggles with food. Brown has argued that anorexic women are not striving to be thin because they suffer from distorted body image, because they can't see how thin they already are. Instead, the reason can be located in our current social relations: a small and thin woman "is beautiful in patriarchy's eyes because she is less visible, and because she occupies a minimum amount of physical space" (Brown 1985, 63). Being minimally muscular and physically weak are further requirements of women's beauty in patriarchal society, as are women's skills to nurture and feed others, especially men, but never themselves. In our social structure, women must avoid gaining power at all cost. Feelings of guilt for nurturing and feeding themselves, feelings of self-hate and self-disgust for being fat ("unfeminine") all act to deprive women of claims to space. Hence, Brown concluded that "... the apparent preoccupation with food and weight of many American women is actually a manifestation of women's struggles to express needs for power and visibility that are denied in a sexist society" (ibid., 67).

Brown's analysis of the interrelationships between weight and issues of power in women's lives offers some new insights into Simone's struggles with food. We recall that as a small child, she ate copious amounts to keep up with her visiting relative. Why? Perhaps that was the only way she had to claim space, to command attention, to be "somebody" in her family. But her experiences as she was growing up taught her that the life of a fat woman is a miserable life, that only thin and pretty girls can claim attention, acceptance and love in patriarchy's eyes. So she dreamed of the day when her life as a princess — slim and pretty — would commence, of the day when she could be allowed to be by *not* taking up space.

But Simone's dream has never been fulfilled. She has been slim, even too slim, but never the princess of men's desires. In fact, she had no time for men; she was too busy thinking and worrying about her weight and what she looked like. Tired of the endless struggle with food, exhausted from the ordeal of fighting for a thin body, Simone wrote in her diary: "I want to be numb so nothing can hurt me.... I don't care about me any more. How worthless and repulsive I feel!"

Simone hoped that, by becoming as thin as she could possibly be, her preoccupation with food would vanish. Losing more weight was seen as the means to drive away the never-ending thoughts about dieting, weight and appearance. It was inconceivable to Simone that she could be thinking about anything other than her weight and appearance. For her, the body has become an object to fight, trick, manipulate and render subservient to an ideal that she was led to believe she had to emulate. The unity of the body *I have* and the body *I am* has been severed under the critical and rejecting gaze of others, by experts who advise women to "become who you *really* are." It is in this split that Simone's and other women's struggle with food can be located.

The commercial weight-loss clinics exploit and also fuel the split that women experience between the bodies they *are* and *have*. They don't tell women of the dangers of dieting. They don't ask why she wants to lose weight in the first place; they simply reassure her that she will, if she signs on the dotted line, pays up and follows the program. They reinforce the view that losing weight — in and of itself — is a good thing. Weight-loss centres are free to offer any services they wish. They are not subject to government regulations; they are limited only in the sale of certain types of weight-loss drugs (Turner 1988, L1, L4). They are free to reduce, squeeze, poke and help starve women to death, as some cases illustrate. They are not held responsible for the consequences of their practices. They don't even have to tell women that 95 percent of them are likely to gain back the weight they may lose in less than a year.

With the assistance of weight-loss clinics, a continuous

splitting is taking place in women's lives as they struggle to perfect their appearance in order to be loved, accepted and successful. For these women, the "fat me" is "not me," for who would want a fat woman? When I asked Simone what it was like for her to talk about herself when she was overweight, it was evident that the time when she was seventy or eighty pounds heavier is not allowed to be part of who she is today. She said,

> No, it's not really [hard]. I don't care about that any more. I really don't think about it. I really don't feel anything, you know. I never really have, except at the time. You know, when I talk about it, it just doesn't really seem like I'm talking about me anyway. So it doesn't really bother me.

A few feminist authors have tried to explain how such splitting of oneself may have come about. Friedman depicts bulimic women as having suffered a "narcissistic injury" (Friedman 1985, 63) in their relationships with their mothers. Because the Self of a child was inadequately mirrored and the emerging self was met with disapproval and rejection, she could not develop a sense of the "real Self" (ibid.). The urges and desires welling up from the Self have come to signify danger, rather than needs and wishes that are part of life. Thus, these strivings are driven underground; they become "not-me"; they are "ego-alien" (ibid., 64).

The regression and splitting of the Self, Friedman also notes, occurs in a climate of widespread "hostility to the totality of the feminine Self" (ibid., 63), in a society that devalues women. The Self that develops is one that is intent on pleasing others and seeks to avoid criticism and hurt at all cost. To heal the splits and to allow the "natural Self" to emerge, Friedman concludes, the woman must confront the "grief and rage of the unmothered child" (ibid., 67). Woodman suggests that the fathers' unconscious devaluation of everything feminine and the rejection of the feminine ego by anorexic women's mothers results in one thing: the "loss of the feminine ego" (Woodman 1980, 101). The loss of the feminine ego manifests itself in the rejection of the feminine body.

Suzy Orbach (1986) has argued that daughters are brought up to be like their mothers; they learn to attend to the needs of others and deny their own needs in this process. Eventually, they become unable to identify their own needs. Despite the mother's ambivalence about her own, compulsory, needless status, mothers must raise girls in this manner, because they need their daughters to be like them. They need their daughters to be pretty — they are often the ones who encourage their daughters in the first place to commence a weight-reduction program.

According to Orbach, the precondition of anorexic development is the "breeding of body insecurity" (p. 70) in women and their development as both objects and consumers in this process. The practices of the relentless pursuit of thinness are aimed at overcoming a profound sense of unentitlement to being in the world. The message surrounding women is one of badness, emptiness and failure in general. The hunger strike of the anorexic woman calls attention to the deprivation and negativity of all women's lives. She merely carries to its limits the struggle to measure up, to feel that she deserves a place in the sun.

Simone attempted, when she was overweight, to ignore her body as much as possible, or to divert attention from it. She said that it was the lack of comments from others about "how nice" she looked that she found hard to live with. As other people came to ignore her appearance, Simone followed suit. When asked what it was like for her to be looking at herself in the mirror before she lost weight, Simone said:

> I didn't do it very often. I would not think about it, just stare at the image long enough to do whatever I had to do: apply make-up and comb my hair. I really tried to avoid mirrors because I looked so enormous, you know. Maybe I wasn't that fat, but it just seemed to me that there wasn't much space between the two sides of the mirror and the reflection. I don't remember anything else I could see other than this big, huge enormous reflection staring back at me, almost taunting me.

Perhaps many other fat women, when they looked in the

mirror, did not like their bodies any more than Simone did, but some of them, in Orbach's "compulsive eaters" groups in *Fat Is a Feminist Issue*, did associate fat with feelings of self-confidence, substance and strength. These women experienced fat as having a kind of power, the power of safety. Fat was seen as providing sexual protection by essentially desexualizing women (in terms of pervasive cultural standards of heterosexual attractiveness). Fat, for these women, was a shell, an armour to keep themselves at a safe distance from men's advances and from sexual harassment.

Unfortunately, however, Orbach's account of her compulsive eaters and her treatment of their eating problem suggests that for her, and for the women in her therapy groups, thin remained the privileged form. The "real self" (for Simone and many other women) was assumed to be contained in a thin body. Diamond, in a critique of Orbach's *Fat Is a Feminist Issue,* argues convincingly that thin, rather than fat, is the feminist issue: Orbach and others have accepted the ideal of thinness as a "natural state" and treated fat as "pathological and a problem" (Diamond 1985, 52). Fat is bad; it should be swapped for one's own real (thinner) body. Diamond notes that, although Orbach emphasizes that a woman had the right to choose whatever shape or size she wanted to be, and although Jane Fonda and Victoria Principal say that women come in a variety of shapes and sizes, in the end all three of them exclude "physical variety ... by narrowing down their emphasis to the ' thin' ideal" (ibid., 4-5).

This is not really surprising when we consider the pervasive pressure all women experience to be thin. The difficulties of opposing thinness at a personal level are highlighted by six fat women who were interviewed by Nopper and Harley (1986). Like bulimarexic women (Boskind-White & White 1983), they spoke of double messages given to them by their physicians. They described the pressures they have experienced to lose weight so that they could find clothes that fit, so that they could be seen as attractive and find the dates they had learned that they must have.

They also spoke of discrimination and contempt even by women acquaintances. They related their astonishment at hearing women say that any illness is preferable to being fat, providing that the illness is accompanied by weight loss. One of the six women described herself as follows:

> I am fat and I am a woman. I weigh 270 pounds. There is no doubt in my mind that I am expected to be thin, to conform to current standards of beauty. The clothing industry and the health care system cater to the needs of thin people who, in turn, stare at my body in disgust....
>
> I have spent most of my life dieting. I have banana and yogurt, egg and grapefruit, "high protein" and "eat all you want and get thin" schemes coming out of my ears and still nothing has ever come off my body....
>
> I have been fat for 46 years. I have just had a physical exam and I'm happy to report that I am in top physical condition .... Still, my physician tells me that I should attend a self-help group for fat people. It includes a diet program that requires a three week food supplement costing $40 a week. The doctor tells me I am physically fit and also tells me that I am unhealthy because I am fat. (Nopper & Harley 1986, 24-26)

Simone did not hear the kinds of double messages this woman described. All she ever heard was that "fat is bad." She was not an "insecure" child in the first place who therefore was particularly bothered by being called "fatty." She came to feel and think about herself in disparaging terms because of the disparaging treatment that fat people, including herself, received. When she was no longer fat, she still thought about herself in disparaging terms — because then she binged and purged to keep her weight down.

When women pursue thinness by binging and purging they may be told, even by those who have practiced weight control using the same method, that they are failures as women. This judgement contradicts our society's widespread positive valuation of self-control manifested in weight control, and it may leave women puzzled and confused. For twenty years Fonda kept secret the fact that "... she suffered from the crippling disease of bulimia." Fonda has stated, "What made me finally stop [binging and purging] was the realization that my life was really important to me and the choice was between being *a good mother and wife* and being a bulimic" (Janos 1985, 170). Bulimia, in the same breath, is designated both as a disease and as a moral failure. Fonda's statement suggests that the bulimic woman is both sick and *bad* — she could not possibly be *"a good mother and wife"* if she were bulimic. Fonda's solution to the moral dilemma caused by being bulimic has been exercise. Working out, rather than binging and purging, now ensures that she remains as "close to the bone" as possible (Diamond 1985, 54). She, with others, has made workout a virtue and a cure for bulimia; she has helped foster the guilt and shame many women in situations similar to Simone's have experienced.

Simone was preoccupied with food and dieting to the exclusion of almost any other concern. She thought about and paid attention to little else aside from how to make herself thin and how to resist temptations to binge. This preoccupation is reflected very clearly in the description of values, norms, ideals and aspirations that follows.

Simone's main project in the last five years of her life has been to avoid being fat. Being fat has meant, without a shadow of doubt, being ugly, repulsive, disgusting, hateful, piggish, grumpy, humiliated and embarrassed. She learned that being fat severely limits one's opportunities. Being fat suggests to others that a person has no self-control, deserves no respect, invites punishment, can be treated merely as a sex object and is worthless, Simone felt.

Being fat has meant for Simone being unhappy, lonely, unloved, living a life of pretenses and smiling even when she does not feel like it. It has meant being a target of teasing or, at best, being ignored by men, receiving no compliments, wondering if others say nice things to avoid hurting the fat person's feelings. It means being an outsider.

Being fat has also meant being unable to look at herself in the mirror, being fed up with herself and resigning herself to a life of unhappiness. It means a woman may never have children and a male partner, for men would be embarrassed to be seen with her, and her children would be ashamed to have a fat mother. Being fat has no rewards.

In Simone's experience, being fat means thinking constantly about food but trying not to; it means always wishing one were thin, going on different diets that do not work, always being disappointed in herself, not feeling comfortable anywhere, not looking good in anything and, generally, having a hopeless life.

> When you're fat you don't realize your limitations. You think that you can look like anybody as long as you lost weight. Perfect, you'd have a perfect body if you just stopped eating and lost weight. You'd instantly become like one of them.

Simone believed that a woman can only be truly happy if she is thin. She was led to believe that through self-control (relentless, rigid dieting), it is possible to lose weight and maintain herself at a low weight. Being thinner for her has meant "getting better," that is, having more self-control, self-worth and dignity. Losing weight is praised by others. If a woman is unable to diet rigidly and persistently, it is better to use any means of weight control (purging by vomiting, abusing laxatives and diuretics) than to allow herself to become fat. She never heard or saw any ideas to the contrary.

Simone learned that the prospect of becoming thinner makes every minute spent not eating worthwhile; it is a great reward for practicing self-control. Even when dining out, it is worth only ordering a salad and nothing else, as Simone did. Being thin affords a woman the opportunity to play hard-to-get with men. It also entitles her to show more openly that she feels sad or angry. Fat women — in Simone's experience — must always look happy.

Simone was taught that professionals and experts are there to help a woman to perfect herself, especially her appearance. Weight-loss clinics can teach her how to lose weight, how to be slim and "healthy." Popular women's magazines try to do much of the same thing; they offer advice on dieting, exercise, fashion and life-style. Fitness clubs offer personalized exercise programs based on one's individual fitness level.

Simone's image of a beautiful princess was one of pleasing others with her appearance. A beautiful princess is liked and admired for the way she looks. She is sweet, caring, fun and has a good sense of humour. She can participate in conversations, and she is not worried about being smart enough. When a woman is not a beautiful princess, she compares her appearance continuously with that of actual or imagined women.

Being a beautiful princess is one example of Simone's striving to be the best. In order to become the best, however, she knew that she also had to work hard, consistently and competitively. She believed that getting good grades was important if she were to have a good job — a job that carries high status.

Striving for the best has also included being a perfect daughter. A perfect daughter "shines"; she is "the pride and joy" of her parents; she is "a success," in Simone's words. She does not make any mistakes. If she does make a mistake, she deserves to be punished. She acknowledges that her parents know what is best for her, and she lives by their rules. She does nothing to embarrass her family. She respects her elders at all times. She is always polite. Furthermore, she tries to look like the rest of her family (not fat if everyone else is thin). She is not selfish or self-centred. She never disappoints her family; she always does everything right.

Simone believed that her wanting to be thin was related to the issue of "who is in control here" — her parents or herself. She said:

It's a feeling of I want to be in control of what I do, and I want to lose weight because that is what I want to do. And I don't care what other people think. That's how I feel.

Simone's words, "I don't care what other people think," contradicts statements she made about why she wanted to be thin. She firmly believed that she would look better weighing 10 pounds less, for example. And, when I asked her if she would consider showing her parents who is "in control" by gaining 10 or even 50 pounds, she said, "No! I would never do that!" She could not achieve her other goal — "a sense of thinness" — that way.

Simone wanted to be thin in order to fit in with the rest of her family and to be loved and accepted by them. She wanted to be fashionable, to be able to feel comfortable wearing any clothes (that are in style) and to be seen as attractive. Through binging and purging she hoped to achieve and maintain a thin body, which she thought was an essential precondition for being loved and accepted.

Simone has learned that there are problems in life, and that the problems in life — like problems in general — have solutions. All one needs to do is recognize this and develop problem-solving skills. Simone believed that if a person did not make the right choice, she alone was to blame for her failure.

Not being perfect has clearly meant for Simone feeling like a failure. Feelings, however, solve nothing. She learned she should not show feelings other than happiness. No matter what her experiences are, she should keep on smiling. Feeling guilty, anxious, frustrated, angry, conflicted, depressed and so forth are worse than feeling numb. She must never allow herself to express to others that she is feeling on the verge of breaking down. In order to avoid pain, to hold herself together, she should keep busy, active and involved in the lives of others. These were the solutions offered to Simone. But activities do not make feelings of loneliness and emptiness vanish. As Simone wrote, "I've been busy and all, but something is definitely missing.... I feel so empty." She may have watched television "to get involved in someone else's life for a change," to forget about her misery, but, when the show was over, she knew that what she wanted to do all along was to have a binge.

We would be hard pressed to suggest that Simone's pursuit of thinness was anything but rational. She has tried to be and do what everyone and everything around her suggested that she should. Her actions have been consistent with the messages, the values, norms, ideals and expectations with which she has been raised. We do not need to probe the depth of her psyche; we do not need to poke for anything that is different than most families' interactions between parents and children; we do not need to look for hidden biochemical imbalances that may have predisposed her toward binging and purging to understand what she has attempted to accomplish and why. As a young, white women living in relative material comfort in Canada, she has only wanted to be loved, accepted and valued as a person, by using the tools that have been offered to her toward this end. As in the case of so many other women in a similar position, who have been raised with the same values, her body has been the vehicle of her search for love and acceptance, for a place in the sun.

A few years ago Simone commenced studies at the university level, but she had to drop out in the first year. It was in that year that she was hospitalized for the third time. Shortly after her discharge from hospital, Simone found a part-time job. At the time of the last interview, she was looking for a permanent full-time position and planned to move out of her parents' house in the near future, into a place of her own.

When these interviews were conducted, Simone was no longer in hospital, but her life continued to focus on her pursuit of thinness to the exclusion of almost any other concern.

In our last interview, Simone said that she still felt hopeless and discouraged most of the time. She believed that she had tried everything suggested to her to break the "vicious cycle" of binging and purging, but nothing had a lasting effect. She saw herself as a "worthless, disgusting person who did not deserve to live." She felt she had nothing to live for — no one to love and no one to love her. Dating and marriage did not appear to occupy her very much. It seemed, she said, that she was still unable to think about anything but food, what she ate, what she shouldn't have eaten, and about how to lose weight. She thought that with the help of another weight-control clinic she could lose 10 pounds, and maybe that could help her to break the cycle of binging and purging.

She thought that it was only when she was satisfied with her appearance — when she no longer *felt* fat — that she could fight the urge to binge and break the cycle. Once she lost the 10 pounds she could continue dieting rigidly, for the rest of her life.

> I just want to be small, that's all. I'm built small. I'm never gonna be big, never gonna be 5'8" and an amazon. I have a very limited amount to work with. *If I want to change anything, the only thing I can change is my body.*

CHAPTER THREE

GOOD GIRLS HAVE IT ALL

LIZ REMEMBERED BEING hungry a lot of the time as a child. Her mother was always policing Liz's and, to a lesser extent, her brothers', eating. She tried to stay away from foods her mother forbade her to eat — cookies, chips, peanuts, cakes and chocolates — because she would get fat and her skin would not be beautiful. Her mother took care of her figure and wanted Liz to do the same.

By the time Liz was fourteen she was convinced that she had to look good. In order to look good, she had to refrain from eating oily foods and sweets. If her mother caught Liz with her hand in the cookie jar or saw her take a piece of cake, she slapped her hand and yelled, "You'll get fat! You'll get pimples!" But since her mother always tried to save money, it was never entirely clear to Liz whether she was against Liz eating these foods because she was concerned about Liz's appearance or because she just wanted her to cost less.

Liz's father was a factory worker; her mother was raised by a well-to-do family. She resented giving up a big house and a comfortable life to follow her restless husband to Canada from Europe. He resented having to support a family, and he was often away for long periods at a time. Where he went, and what he did away from the family, Liz did not know. When he was at home during weekends, he drank heavily.

Liz's mother looked after the children and earned money to make the mortgage payments on the house. She farmed a piece of land from which most of their food came, and she sold some of the produce. She struggled a great deal to make ends meet. In Liz's family only her father — the designated bread winner — wore new clothes or had fresh milk to drink. The rest of the family had milk made from powder and dressed from used clothing stores. In her husband's absence, Liz's mother had affairs. Whenever both parents were at home, verbal fights were a frequent occurrence.

When Liz's girlfriend announced that she was going on a diet, Liz thought that she should do the same. Although Liz had not considered herself fat before, she believed that she should also lose weight since she was heavier than her girlfriend. More than anything else, Liz wanted to be attractive and popular and have dates:

> I was starting to become more aware of my appearance. Instead of just doing sports for sports' sake I was exercising to look good. I wanted to be noticed by the boys because all the girls were starting to want to be noticed by the boys. I was reading books on how to be popular with boys, how to look good. And, of course, my mother was getting these books on the menstrual cycle and they tell you how to take care of yourself, use deodorant, brush your teeth, wash your hair.

Wanting to be popular brought Liz into conflict with her parents and with herself. As a child she was not allowed to spend much time with friends, other children were not permitted to come home to play with her. When Liz was in junior high school, dating and wearing make-up were forbidden. Until age eleven — often for her brothers' mischiefs — Liz's mother strapped her frequently as punishment. Liz felt at the time that her mother hated her for looking like her father and for knowing about the affairs she had in her husband's absence. Her father wanted Liz to be a good student, to "use her brain," to be conversant on many subjects, to be "somebody," and her mother especially wanted her to "marry a rich man." They both wanted her to earn and save money for her education; they wanted her to learn that she had to pay for everything she wanted. It was clear to Liz that her family's resources were too scarce to help her achieve the desired image.

Liz was a very ambitious and a good student. She was active in Sunday school and in sports; she did a paper route to earn pocket money; she picked up after her brothers and father, planned the family's meals, cooked and baked and served "endless pots of tea" for her parents.

Wanting to be popular was also in conflict with Liz's own stated desire "to be first, to be the top all the time." She was "too good" as a student ("a brown noser"), she was "too good" in sports, but she was not popular with boys. She came to realize that she could not be the outstanding student she was, especially in math, and have dates at the same time.

That first diet lasted two weeks. Liz binged for the first time before this diet and for the second time at the end of the two weeks. For the next seventeen years, Liz binged and purged and dieted with few breaks in between.

At that time, age fourteen, Liz stopped doing sports for the enjoyment of it, and became very concerned with looking like a perfect woman: attractive and beautiful. She began to concentrate on how to become more popular. She sought to be in the limelight, participated in the school's drama group, and got herself on the school's public announcement system, waiting to be noticed and discovered by boys. But, there was always another girl who was considered more attractive, was cast in a more desirable role in the school's play, was more humorous, wittier or prettier. It seemed to Liz that she was forever comparing herself and competing with other girls, and not once did she feel that she measured up, that she was number one. Liz learned that women must be competitive. The prettiest looking one has the best chance of being popular with men. She should be number one in everything she does, Liz heard over and over again. If she cannot be number one in an activity, she should not do it at all.

Liz knew that there was more to popularity and to being number one (most wanted by boys) than having an attractive body. She noticed that the most popular girls were also "easy" with boys, and this too created a conflict for her. She believed in love and in saving herself for the man she was going to marry. She could not resolve these issues, but continued to read a great deal on the subject of popularity with boys and attempted to put into practice what she had read:

> I remember reading that girls should let boys do all the talking. Smile and say nice things to a boy, cliché things ... like, "Michael, what big muscles you have!" ... Although I would not have said anything as silly as that, I may have said, "Oh, you have such a nice smile," or "you're so smart!" ... I was supposed to sit and listen and smile at everything HE said, and never be bored or look bored ....

From their earliest years, girls learn that they are less important than boys. They are expected to help out others but ask for nothing for themselves. By the time they grow up to be women, they have learned to always take second place, to let men take the biggest and best parts of a meal (Delphy 1984), to let them do most of the talking (Spender 1980), "to agree with men" and to avoid getting them upset (Cline & Spender 1987, 38). At school, girls continue to learn to be silly or silent so as to maintain men's feelings of superiority (Howe 1976). They learn to let men interrupt them — for whatever it is they are engaged in cannot be as important as a man's question, comment or tirade. Taking second place in eating, talking and any other activity comes down to taking up less space; it is a constriction of territory that a girl or a woman can call her own. In learning to take up less space (both literally and figuratively) we forgo learning that we have rights — as persons and as women.

The books and magazines Liz and other women read were filled with instructions on "how to get a man" and "how to keep a man." Looking good, being affectionate and giving and pleasing men in every way possible way were among the requirements women had to fulfil in order to get and keep a man. If they wanted to be noticed and asked for a date, they had to be of the shape and size gentlemen preferred. Women were told never to initiate contact, let alone ask for a date with a man; she must wait for him to speak to her first and to ask her out. Women were also told that to attract men who are rich and successful it is helpful to know what the man's favourite past-times are and for the women to become fairly competent in these activities.

It is worth looking in some detail at what women's magazines have been telling their readers and also what they have been silent about. In a study of British women's magazines, Ferguson (1983) found that the dominant themes of these magazines remained rather constant from the late 1940s to the early 1980s. For decades, they have instructed women in the "cult of femininity," based on the assumption that "... a female sex which is at best unconfident, and at worst incompetent, 'needs' or 'wants' to be instructed, rehearsed or brought up to date on the arts and skills of femininity" (p. 2). According to Ferguson, one of the most striking features of these magazines is that they treat women as if they were bound together by their biological sex with no major differences among them and, simultaneously, as if women were set apart from the world except for what has been defined for them as their concerns. A sense of "us together" has been fostered by these magazines when, in fact, popular women's magazines offer little to no information to their readers about the lives of women who are not middle class, white or, in the case of Ferguson's 1983 study, British.

Women's situations outside Canada and the United States are similarly excluded as subject matter from the contents of popular women's magazines in Canada. These magazines, much like the mass media in general, continue to propagate stereotyped and idealized images of white, urban, upper-middle class or upper class existence, as if this was all women's reality (Wilson 1976). I examined forty-six issues of thirteen different women's magazines mentioned by the interviewed women, which were published between 1981 and 1985, and I was left with the distinct impression that women are hardly encouraged to learn about women's varied situations and concerns in this country and elsewhere. The magazines included several issues of *Chatelaine*, *City Woman*, *Cosmopolitan*, *Seventeen*, *Mademoiselle*, *Glamour*, *Self*, *New Woman*, *Ladies' Home Journal*, *McCalls*, *Vogue*, *Images* and *Redbook*. There was only one article that contained more than a few words about women's (and men's as well as children's) living conditions on another continent (*Ladies' Home Journal* May 1984). But even this article focused more on Mother Teresa, "the world's most admired woman," than on the local situation in which Mother Teresa worked. In the travel section of one magazine, there was one sentence depicting the way in which women in a foreign country dress and the work they do for a living (*Vogue* July 1981). This description was included as an illustration of the "exotic" character of this country that is a "must" for travellers. In an editorial, bearing the title "Uncommon Facts and Figures That Capture the Changing Roles and Rules of Women's Lives at the Close of 1984" (*Glamour* Dec. 1984), the percentages of women legislators and women in the supreme court of the U.S.S.R. and the U.S.A. were quoted, and in a few of the magazines there were pictures of Asian, South or Central American children — crying or smiling — for advertisements of foster parents' plans (e.g., *Self* Feb. 1985). Needless to say, there was no analysis of why these children need North American foster parents, nor why there are so many (or so few) women in supreme courts in the U.S.S.R. and the U.S.A. This is the extent to which the forty-six magazines introduced information about women's lives outside of our continent.

The magazines' treatment of women's varied situations in North America was also utterly inadequate. Articles on issues of concern to most North American women rarely appeared on these pages. In the forty-six magazines, there was only one article on day care (*Chatelaine* March 1982) one on women's pensions (*Chatelaine* May 1982), and one on part-time work for women (*Chatelaine* Oct. 1981). These issues and many others, which were not even alluded to in the magazines, are of grave concern to large numbers of women, but they seem to have no place in women's magazines. Finally, there was not a single article that as much as mentioned the particular problems and conflicts of Black, Native Indian or immigrant women, working-class women, poor women, single mothers, lesbians, prostitutes.

In a study of fictional and profiled heroines in Canadian women's magazines (*Chatelaine* and *Maclean's*) between 1930 and 1970, S. Wilson (1977) also argues that women's diverse situations had not been represented adequately:

> Fiction magazine heroines were not employed in the Blue Collar, Primary, Transportation or Service sectors of the economy, although approximately one-half of the female labour-force are.... Professionals and Managers were over-represented and unglamorous jobs were virtually ignored. Profile heroines were employed in a wide range of occupations, most of which were high-status, important, stimulating and often highly rewarded .... (p. 41)

> The messages transmitted by fiction and profile in Canadian mass magazines were often conflicting. Profiles were generally about women who were successful occupationally and whose success was not hampered by ethnic background, education or by decisions to marry or have children. On the other hand, the remuneration and prerequisites accompanying high status jobs mean that role-conflicts are more easily managed. The life-style accompanying the job of an actress, a politician or a member of the royal family is remote from the life-experiences of most Canadian women. (Wilson 1976, 43)

Issues of *Chatelaine* from the past three years continue to offer the traditional women's columns (fashion, beauty, food, decorating, crafts, child care and health) and introduce successful or famous women, but contain little information and no analysis about most women's everyday problems and conflicts. Although it is true that there are alternative feminist publications whose goal is to present material for critical reflection, their circulation is much more limited than that of *Chatelaine*. This latter magazine plus *Cosmopolitan*, *Glamour* and *Mademoiselle* are the ones that most women in this country, including those interviewed for this study, have been reading. Girls and women learn what *should* be their issues and concerns from these magazines; these are invariably their appearance, being good lovers, mothers, wives — and, more recently, career women.

At age fifteen, Liz started to rebel. She was fed up with trying to do the right thing but never succeeding at it. There had been many activities in which Liz wanted to participate, but didn't because her parents refused permission by screaming and yelling — "teaching about priorities." She was told to work and study as hard as she could in order to gain admission to university. When she asked if she could take ballet classes, she was told they were too expensive and not part of the curriculum. Eventually she learned to "sneak" the activities she knew her parents would not sanction, such as sports, dating and using make-up. She was so embarrassed about the second-hand clothes she wore that sometimes she stole dresses to look more like the other girls at school.

Liz stopped telling her parents about her activities; she stopped asking and begging for their permission. One day, when she was half an hour late getting home, her father hit her so hard that she was knocked across the room. He told her to leave the house if she was not going to "live by the rules." She picked up her belongings and did not return home for three years.

When Liz left home she worked full-time to support herself, and she continued with her studies. She took dance classes, attended a finishing course and dated regularly. She worked very hard, paying for all her expenses, including the finishing course, and even saved some money for her university education. She enjoyed her new life and also took pleasure in impressing people with how much she could fit into a day. She also began advising other girls on hair-do, make-up and style of appearance in general. Her words suggest that she understood:

> The real objective was to be the prettiest girl. The competition is tough. You've got to dress nice; you've got to wear make-up, you know, make yourself the best you can be.

The "best," without doubt, meant the most attractive, but what was considered the most attractive changed during Liz's teens. When she was fourteen-fifteen, the girl in the school who was regarded as the most attractive had a "voluptuous body with big breasts and small waist, but she was also solid," Liz explained. "She was a gymnast." Liz, on the other hand, felt that she "looked like a boy ... straight up and down, ... flat with no curves." Within three years, however, Liz's body became more voluptuous as well, but by then "thin was in" — a fashionable woman's body had to have angular lines. Liz then became jealous of girls who "could eat and eat and eat and never gain weight." Liz's struggle for being slim, in order to become more popular, had begun.

A conversation that Kim Chernin recorded in the sauna of a fitness club amply illustrates women's struggle with slimness. This conversation took place between two women; one "very beautiful, the sort Renoir would have admired," the other a white-haired, tanned woman of about sixty with a boyish figure. The "plump" one said, "I've heard about that illness, anorexia nervosa, ... and I keep looking around for someone who has it. I want to sit next to her. I think to myself, maybe I'll catch it ...." (Chernin 1981, 22). I have heard almost the same words from women who have been struggling with their weight. Garner (1983b) has reported that many women clients were disappointed when they were told their diagnosis was *not* anorexia nervosa. These statements point to women having internalized the objectification of their bodies by others and having come to objectify both their own bodies and the bodies of other women. The body is reduced to a specific shape and size, and achieving this particular body form becomes the most important goal in the lives of many women, including Liz.

Pretty has become equated with being slim for Liz, as for most women, men and children surrounding her. Having a thin body, however, was not sufficient for a girl to be considered attractive and asked out on dates. She needed to have "well manicured nails, nice legs, clear skin, not a hair out of place" — a "model" appearance. Liz said she believed that "appearance was all encompassing and it was the most important aspect of a girl's life," so she enrolled in the Nancy Taylor finishing course to perfect her knowledge on the subject. Here Liz learned more about make-up, about how to walk, sit, talk, entertain and do everything a model does as prescribed. She learned more about how to appear "smart" in the company of men. Part of being smart was to "speak only when spoken to." When the man talks, she must look directly at him and smile all the time. It is, of course, not permissible for a woman ever to look annoyed, angry, bored or frustrated. She has to feed a man well — "the way to a man's heart is through his stomach," Liz said. Furthermore, she has to listen to everything he says with "bated breath" and never show boredom, anger or disagreement.

Psychologists in the advertising industry have lent their expertise to what comes down to the oppression and exploitation of women (and men). Liz was also instructed in this through the finishing course. Renowned media psychologists, such as Dr. Joyce Brothers, have made their contribution to this state of affairs. For decades she has been telling women how to make themselves into anything and everything others want them to be, including how to work off (by exercise) their bad temper should they develop a "case" of it. She and others have told women over and over again that their responses to difficult situations, such as compulsive eating, have been maladaptive, that they need better coping strategies. Women's magazines are full of these messages as well. Acquiring know-how, (time management, stress management, classes on how to eat right) is the answer offered again and again to what are defined as "problems." The experts' advice often amounts to reducing human conflicts that are rooted in the socio-economic and political realms of existence to psychological management, which offers women prescriptions against rebellion. For example, if a woman is refused a job because she is seen as old, the answer Brothers gives to her is to buy a face-lift:

> No woman has "earned" sagging jowls, puffiness under the eyes, drooping eyelids, wrinkles, a crepey neck and all the rest. They are the result of the force of gravity and the wear and tear of life. There is no reason why we should not smooth and lift our faces just as we reupholster an expensive sofa — tightening its sagging springs, adding fresh padding where necessary and covering it with a beautiful new fabric.
>
> If you have the money, there is no reason why you should not spend it on a face-lift if that is what you want, just as there is no reason why you should not remodel your kitchen if that is what you want. (Brothers 1975, 100-101)

Brothers' graphic comparison of a woman's face with a sofa and kitchen could itself be the subject of a fascinating analysis as a prime example of objectification. But, to return to her advice: if "business favors youth," women must fight discrimination by the individual purchasing of youth. The woman who cannot afford the face-lift, but needs a job to survive, is not Brothers' concern. It does not seem to occur to Brothers that other courses of action might be necessary to battle business' favouring of youth. In the same flippant manner, Brothers addresses the question of women seeking "a new image": it means simply acquiring a new hair style or a new eye colour — "if you feel that would add to your general well-being" (ibid., 110). But this new image must be considered as carefully, she says, as buying a great painting or a new house. Brothers advises women to study carefully contemporary fashion magazines, both for clothing and general appearance. For maximum efficiency and easy reference, women should accumulate a file of hairstyles to take to a reputable hair dresser for consultation.

Then, there is a host of free, or almost free, ways of achieving a new image. Anyone who does not take advantage of these "miraculous beautifiers" that "cost nothing — or practically nothing" (p. 113) — should be spanked, says Brothers:

> There is no excuse for a dirty neck, dirty, dandruffy hair, for dirty nails, for hairy legs. There is no excuse for body odor. I am aware that some young women feel that unshaven legs, a gamey smell, lank and oily hair are an expression of liberation. I disagree. These women are isolating themselves from society — just the opposite of liberation. This lack of respect for one's body reflects a more serious lack of respect for one's self.... Lack of care for one's body is a generally accepted sign of emotional disturbance. (Brothers 1975, 119)

Simply put, nonconformity, especially nonconformity to "free" methods of what is deemed self-care, equals craziness. My gut-level response to such advice, particularly in the name of what's in women's best interests (as Joyce Brothers claims), is sheer fury.

Citations about "well-intended" advice to women could continue almost endlessly. The message that comes through in so much of the advice given through the media is stated very clearly once again by Brothers:

> Beauty is far from a frivolous subject. In our society, if you don't look your best, forget it. The best jobs, the highest pay, the most interesting opportunities and — usually — the most desirable men go to the most attractive women. (pp. 128-129)

As we look at Liz's life in the 1960s in a small town in Ontario, we find that many of the values, norms of behaviour, ideals and images, goals and aspirations she learned are the same as those propagated in the popular media. She learned that she had to be a good girl and impress others, that she should strive for a full/fulfilled life, be healthy, look good, be attractive. Having money and "catching the right man" — a phrase Liz used — were the most important goals. In order to achieve these goals, she had to be smart, popular, competitive and also present herself as potentially a competent wife and mother.

Liz learned that a woman must have the look that is "in." In her early teens this was the "sweet look." In her later teens, she learned that a woman should look "classy" as well; she has to have nice long legs, attractively chiseled features, and, generally, her appearance should be most like that of a mannequin and a dancer of utmost grace and beauty. A woman must always work at her appearance, for this is her most important asset.

When she was seventeen, Liz got an offer to work as a dancer in a bar, and this offer was followed by several others. She enjoyed many aspects of the job. Besides having become a better-paid worker, she was adored as a dancer, she was good, and men came from far away to see her. She could create her own numbers and her costumes — it was "fun"; it was a challenge; and, as she put it, this work also held the promise of "being discovered" and "making it big." She liked being on stage. Despite the admiration and attention she enjoyed, Liz was determined to observe the rule she had learned about not getting sexually involved with men. She was "saving" herself, as she put it, for the man with whom she was in love and for the wedding they were planning together.

Liz wanted to study, to have her own (preferably well-paying) job as well as to be married and have children. As we have seen, Boskind-Lodahl described similar aspirations among her bulimarexic clients. They wanted to live out their "mother's roles," to be wives and mothers and intimate partners to men, in addition to achieving academically. But, unlike the women in Boskind-Lodahl's groups, Liz's academic and career aspirations were *not* to be forgotten after marriage. Likely, because she had her mother's life as an example, Liz expected that she would have to support herself and possibly her family even after she got married. Liz, like other working-class women, saw that her mother also had to work in a paid job, and she expected to do the same. Although having a career or a family may have appeared as "choices" for Boskind-Lodahl's bulimarexic women, it seems to me that for Liz having a family *and* her own work and her own money were a necessity. However, Liz may have seen this situation as a matter of desire or choice at the time, for her words were that she "wanted it all": family, university, her own work and her own money.

By "wanting it all," Liz may have been ahead of her time, at least ahead of the media messages women received in the 1960s. Ferguson found that between 1949 and 1974 women were told consistently that their main jobs were to make themselves more attractive in order to get and keep their man and to have a happy family. They were also told that, if they were to be good mothers, they must not work outside the home. After 1974, however, the British women's magazines started to tell their readers that a "working" woman (a woman working in the paid labour force) could now also be a good mother and wife, and there was more rhetoric about women's freedom to choose among competing and often contradictory images (Ferguson 1983, 189). The messages about attracting and pleasing men remained essentially the same.

The conditions into which Liz was born offered her a set of rather limited material possibilities for arranging her life and for seeing herself as a certain kind of woman. Both the domain of her identity and her possibilities have been demarcated for and by her along lines of gender and socio-economic differences. However, Liz, like any other woman, has not simply been a "passive subject." As Walkerdine (1984) argues, girls do not adapt passively to female role models; rather, they struggle and reach some solution to a set of conflicts and contradictions that are located in social relations, including those of the family. While the conflicts and contradictions were numerous, it is clear that for Liz, as for most adolescent girls, the conflict-ridden main goal was to attract and keep a boy (McRobbie 1978).

Recalling her life story, Liz noted time and again that her life had been an ongoing instruction in the lesson: a woman's appearance is her major asset. "Using her brain" made her less popular with boys and kept her from competing with other girls for dates — the necessary means to secure a man. Paradoxically, even her rebellion against her parents' rule prompted her to conform to another set of rules: the rules and practices of being feminine. But the origin of these rules and the consequences of conforming to the ideal of feminine appearance, including a particular body, were not visible to Liz. It was only after many years of pain and struggle that she began to question the practices she worked so hard to master.

The notion of the ideal body propagated by the popular media is bound up intricately, albeit not solely, with forms of economic organizations that must create needs and markets for their goods in order to extract profit. It is, "after all, the ideal body that every beauty product manufacturer is selling" (*Ideas* 1983, 28). Shortly after the turn of this century, the cosmetics industry decided that what they were selling to people was a "youthful ideal," rather than beauty per se (Ewen 1976). The sales force was taught that they were going to sell "every artificial thing there is.... And above all things it is going to be young - young - young! We make women feel young" (Woodward 1926, 314). In the 1920s, and ever since then, women have been sold "youth" in all kinds of mass-produced goods: from Palmolive and Resinol soaps through Nujol feminine douche to Sun Maid Raisins, everything promised a clear, radiant, youthful complexion, the looks of a school girl (Ewen 1976). Youth has been equated with pride, confidence and, above all, desirability. "The first duty of a woman is to attract" (Ewen 1976, 132), and they were promised that their duty would be fulfilled by having a youthful appearance.

Ewen (1976) recounts how women have been made to feel guilty and inadequate in the hope that they would purchase the goods offered to them to get rid of these feelings. Advertisers began to photograph women with mirrors in hand or near them; even in the kitchen there had to be one so that they could quickly "correct the imperfections" in their appearance. Women have been taught to see themselves externally, as objects, competing against other women who also view themselves as objects of men's desires. They have been made self-conscious about their bodies, and temporary relief from this self-consciousness was offered by consumer goods. Today women are sold not only creams, soaps and perfumes, but also vast amounts of diet pills, laxatives, diuretics, one-calorie pop and diet foods. The claim is made that these products will bring health, pleasure, joy and beauty to all the women who use them. Besides these products, women are offered a wide range of weight-reduction programs and fitness classes that also promise to make women feel youthful, healthy, attractive as well as successful and happy. Chernin (1981) cited a number of more drastic measures that have been made available to women in case the more benign ones fail to bring about the desired end. These measures include, but are not limited to, intestinal bypass surgery, surgical buttocks reduction, thigh shrinking and belly flattening, each for $3,000 U.S. and up.

No single ad, soap opera, movie, women's magazine or newspaper article in isolation teaches women how to feel, think and act, what to value, what to want. It is the conglomeration and the inescapable presence of the messages conveyed that shapes women's situation. All these materials perform ideological, political and economic functions. They foster an "individualized consumer mentality" (Dyer 1982, 110) and produce what women "want." Together "... they *define* what is style and what is good taste, not as possibilities or suggestions, but as unquestionably desirable goals. The world of the ads is the world of the carefree and well-off as seen through the eyes of the advertisers" (Dyer 1982, 13).

Television ads do not present a great variety of possible images of women. Most women are depicted in the home, doing household chores or busying themselves with achieving a certain look — dyeing their hair, using a particular brand of soap or lotion to obtain "silky-soft skin," putting on body spray or a new brand of pantyhose in the hope of attracting the admiring gaze of men.

Those portrayed in the home are typically made to look less attractive than the women outside the home. The women shown outside the home project an image of having infinite fun and constantly receiving men's admiration. They are shown, for instance, dancing in front of the elevators of what is probably a large corporation, where mostly men are the executives, or as a young white beauty sipping chilled white wine from a tall-stemmed glass in an elegant restaurant over candlelight dinner in the company of a handsome male. But even the house-bound women usually have their hair done neatly, wear stylish outfits and are quite young. The women outside the home are always very young and model-like, and, even when they are depicted in a paid-work setting, they do not appear to be working. The settings always suggest affluent and high-status jobs. We do not see women in factories or cleaning ladies in office buildings, many of whom are Women of Colour or immigrant women, working the night shift with varicose veins on their legs from years of labour. The systematic exclusion of women working these jobs (which so many do) suggests the concerted denial of women's varied situations, of the harsh conditions of most women's lives, as well as of the wide range of women's bodies and differences in their appearance. The promises that advertisers make when selling their products could be called into question more easily (and perhaps the products would not sell so well) if women's lives were portrayed more realistically.

Liz could have worked in jobs where attractiveness was not a prime qualification. She had, in fact, had such jobs (cashier, for example). But she quickly learned that as a cashier she could not make enough money to support herself and save for her university education. In addition to offering the opportunity to become more knowledgeable, a university education served the purpose of attracting "higher-calibre" men, men who seemed to have the potential to become successful and wealthier than Liz's own family. Dancing, which Liz started to do part-time while she maintained her cashier job, paid much better. She was adored as a dancer, and this work also held the possibility of success and wealth. Liz could not have been a dancer had it not been for the body she had, a body that could be put on display, that satisfied the taste of the time, that men were willing to pay to see. Liz's body was a commodity, the thing she could exchange directly for a living, rather than indirectly, through being married to a man who was willing to support her. With only the pay cheque of a cashier and no other means of support, Liz would have faced a life of poverty — a life which she was raised to believe that she could avoid by working hard. All her life she heard she could and should do better; she was smart and attractive, and happiness and success were up to her. Although erroneous, this belief in the inevitable success of one's life if one is really determined to work and struggle seems to be shared by most people in North America. Women's bodies are a major site and object of daily work and struggle. It is through working on their bodies that historically women have had a degree of influence. This "power through the body" (Szekely 1987, 43) has been a means of women resisting certain intolerable situations. Simultaneously, it has been the site of their domination and of their objectification — first by others, later by themselves. Women have not been merely passive subjects — victims of "forces of socialization." They have participated in their own oppression (and exploitation), as well as in the (hetero)sexualization of their bodies. Liz knew very well that her body was her means of livelihood and the ground of her identity. She was less clear, however, that in this process she was damaging her body and fostering a split between the body she *was* and the body she *had* (Merleau-Ponty 1962).

At eighteen, Liz moved back home. She was exhausted from working — now in two jobs — and studying, and, when her mother asked her to return, she welcomed the change. But life at home turned out to be "worse than ever." The rules were even stricter than before; the fights were even more intense between the parents. Liz was not permitted to see her fiancé, and all her savings were taken from her. She was tense and anxious much of the time, found herself unable to eat and started losing weight. At first she was pleased with her slimming figure — she described herself as having become "more voluptuous" over the years. By graduation from high school Liz, standing 5′9″ tall, weighed less than seventy pounds, and soon she was hospitalized.

This was almost twenty years ago. Diagnoses of anorexia were rarely made then, and Liz was not ascribed this label. As a working-class girl, Liz was even less likely to be seen as anorexic. To the extent that anorexia nervosa was known at all, in the 1960s it was considered an upper-class disease.

Although exact figures are not available, clinical reports from the 1980s suggest that the number of anorexic patients from the lower socio-economic strata have increased (Garner 1983b; Garner 1983c).

> Until recently, the victims of anorexia nervosa were almost exclusively upper-middle-class adolescent girls. In the past several years, however, because of more inclusive reporting and more accurate diagnosis — and what is generally accepted by experts as an enormous increase in the incidence of the disease itself — the spectrum has been expanded to encompass all socioeconomic levels (though still 97 percent white). (Levenkron 1982, 1)

At present it is not known whether the larger numbers of anorexics from the working class represent a larger percentage of the overall anorexic population, or whether their proportion has remained relatively unchanged as the incidence of eating disorders has increased across *all* social classes. Researchers working with smaller numbers of bulimic women in non-university settings find that these women's class background varied greatly (Lazerson 1982; Szekely & Morris 1986). Boskind-White and White note as well that bulimarexia "appeared rampant not only in the colleges but also in metropolitan areas and isolated rural communities. Housewives, teenagers, and professional women were thereby added to our original population" (Boskind-White & White 1983, 22). The age range for the eating disorders has also widened; it now includes girls younger than ten and women in their sixties and over.

The age range as well as the socio-economic strata for anorexia nervosa and bulimia may have broadened in recent years. We may also be witnessing a trend toward increasing proportions of male anorexics and bulimics (at present 5-10 percent of all anorexics and 10-15 percent of all bulimics are estimated to be men). Still, these disorders continue to be viewed by many clinicians as predominantly white, young, upper-middle class and female conditions that are most prevalent in North America and Western Europe. This perception contributes to the lack of attention that working-class girls and women who relentlessly pursue thinness have received.

Although there are many indications that the phenomenon is no longer a class-bound one, it is rarely asked why this should be the case. How do we explain that anorexia and bulimia have become "more democratic" (Currie n.d.)? It may be that a decade or so ago the media images and messages of thinness (and the promises associated with them) started to proliferate to such a degree and in such a persuasive manner that women who had been able to ignore these promises as clearly beyond their reach could no longer do so. Although many of the tools of achieving a thin and attractive body are very expensive and continue to be available mostly to women of wealth, those with lesser means may be able to afford at least some of the relatively inexpensive diet aids or cheaper fitness facilities that are likely to have been created precisely for their consumption. Aids that make them believe that some day they, too, can be happy, loved, successful or powerful.

Although women have known for a long time "that beauty was coin in the male realm, that beauty translated directly into power because it meant male admiration, male alliance, male devotion" (Dworkin 1974, 36), it is only with the advent of the mass media that large segments of the female population can be promised male admiration, alliance and devotion; hence, security. It is only with the assistance of mass media that the *pursuit* of thinness could be made attractive (and imperative) to Liz and other working-class women. The importance of being thin was described by Liz very succinctly when, pointing at pictures of herself at varying shapes and sizes, she said: "I hated myself when I was fat, and I was in love with myself when I was thin."

By eating the prescribed amounts of food, Liz gained enough weight to be discharged after a few months in hospital. Instead of returning home, however, she moved to a nearby city, where she was to commence her university studies. Within a few months, she found herself with no money. She was not well enough to study and to work to support herself, and her parents refused to return her savings. This circumstance forced her to work part-time, and eventually she quit school. She was again binging, and she started gaining back the weight she had lost the year before. Once more she was offered a dancing job and, shortly after she started dancing again, Liz was raped by a gang.

Liz had attempted to resolve the conflicts and contradictions she experienced as a girl in her mid-teens by pretending she had "no brains" and by becoming very concerned with her appearance to attract men. When she started dancing, she risked being looked upon as a "cheap woman," but she believed in (romantic) love, in no sex without love, in saving herself for the man with whom she was in love. Her vision of romantic love (which included being a virgin) and happiness was shattered when the gang of men broke the lock on her door, while she was taking a shower after work, and raped her. It was not, of course, the rape that made Liz bulimarexic. She had already dieted and binged and had lost so much weight that she had to be hospitalized. Before she returned to dancing, men were not offering to support her; it was only after the rape that a number of men offered to "save the poor soul" by loving and marrying her.

Liz's body, when she was a dancer, was clearly treated as a sexual object. No matter what rules she tried to set for herself (no sex till marriage), it was beyond her power to live by them. When she was raped after work by a whole gang of men, her body became her instrument to forget what had happened to her. She escaped to drugs, alcohol, sex and, later, in an attempt to go straight, to food.

Liz's twenty-year struggle with food and dieting can be understood in the context of a situation in which a woman's work is tied to her sexuality and her worth is defined by her appearance for men's sexual use. Over a hundred years ago Victoria Woodhall tried to tell her female audience about "the sexual and economic system built on their bodies" (Dworkin 1983, 59). In this system, a woman could be "good" (inviolable) by being a wife, and "bad" (violable) by being a prostitute. Liz clearly wanted to be inviolable, but she was perceived at least by the men in the gang as violable. Whether good or bad, women have been subservient to men's presumed sexual needs and to the profit motive of the economic structure in which they live. Throughout history, an attractive and compliant woman has had a better chance of earning or having more — being given more — *by* men.

For Katrina, Simone and Liz — and for Martha, whose story is yet to be told — it was absolutely vital to the realization of their goals (romantic love, happiness, success — in the most general terms) to have a body that would be noticed and desired, otherwise they would be "nothing" and "nobody." Weight control was seen as the necessary means of achieving a desirable body —a body desirable to men. The struggle with food is part of the work of becoming attractive, but the struggle is not — or not merely — about eating. Food/eating is, rather, the arena in which conflicts around a number of issues are played out. Many of these issues involve sexuality — the domination of women's bodies by men's desires — and the profit motive. Posed in a somewhat different way, the question is, who is in control of women's lives? Whose life — by whose standards — is a woman to live?

After a period of escape to drugs, alcohol and sex, Liz decided that she had to begin to take charge of her life again and that she had to try to live a straight life without the help of men. She quit dancing, moved and ate until she weighed over two hundred pounds. Thoroughly disgusted with herself at this point, Liz started a strict diet and exercise regime. Adhering to this regime, in a few months she managed to get her weight down to what she considered acceptable for her. The weight loss meant that she was once more beginning to like herself.

Even though Liz wanted to go straight, and without men's assistance, she could not stop seeing herself through the lens of what constituted attractiveness for women at the time. She could not (nor did she want to) put behind her all she had learned about femininity from magazines, books, television, finishing school and elsewhere. This was the case because, for a woman to be concerned about her body's appearance is, in our society, to be concerned with the possibility of her future existence. Women's pursuit of attractive appearance is an expression of women's attempt to have a future. It is this chord — the anxiety about the future — that the call to perfect our bodies touches, whether or not women are consciously aware of their appearance being a key to their future. Women's pursuit of an attractively feminine body reveals their situations as tied centrally to their relationships with men.

It was clear to Liz that a woman's objective should be to marry a man who is rich and successful. School (university) might be a place where she could meet men who are either already rich, and on their way to being successful, or seem to have the promise of both. To attract such men a woman must be very attractive and also smart. She must have an education. It will prepare her for a better-paying job and also make men of "promise" accessible to her. And, through marriage to a "higher-calibre" man, she can do better than her parents — especially her mother. She must know, however, that she must not be too smart; she must not show that she knows more than the men in her life, and she must accept the help men offer to her.

Being too smart, getting good grades in the sciences or being a good student in general is unpopular among peers, particularly among boys, as Liz found out. In order to belong to a group of popular women, she must not be too different; she must blend into that group. She must take part in the events and activities of this group; she must be extroverted, but not too self-confident — this would intimidate others. She must be "easy" with men so that men would not fear her turning them down for a date. Generally, she should be friendly and smile a lot.

For Liz, having a full/fulfilled life was also a major aspiration. For a woman to enjoy a sense of fulfilment, she must be loved by a man. Travelling and meeting interesting people are further aspects of having a full life. Liz learned as well that it is good to be able to eat and drink as much as we want and whatever we want. Yet, as she realized later in her life, no amount of food, alcohol, drug or sex can give one a lasting sense of fulfilment.

Liz learned many more "dos" and "do nots" that, as a child and adolescent, shaped her actions, the ways she perceived and felt about herself and other people. These "dos" and "do nots" are remarkably (but not surprisingly) similar for all the interviewed women.

These are, of course, ideals that are full of conflicts and contradictions and utterly impossible to realize. It is not possible to be both a good student and a popular girl, as Liz recognized quite early in her life. It is not possible to be a good girl, as defined by the rules of one authority and to be part of the peer group of popular girls. It is also unlikely that a woman can be both popular and number one, since competition for first place involves a process in which friendships are often damaged or altogether sacrificed.

Regarding the importance of attractive appearance we come across another contradiction. Slight variations from the image that women are coaxed to achieve is not encouraged. There is a *particular* appearance they must have, and from that norm they must not deviate. "Norm," however, is a misnomer here; the norm surrounding women is one that nobody lives up to, not even the fashion models presenting us with the image. This notion was clearly illustrated by the movie, *Killing Us Softly*. The image presented in the magazine or television advertisement is the result of the concentrated effort of a crew of experts using various resources to produce a photographable image that is going to sell, not so much a particular item in the advertisement, but, rather, a fantasy that is going to keep us consuming.

The image of a working woman as presented to us is one of youth, slimness and beauty, impeccable appearance in general, simple but expensive-looking clothing, perfect hair and nails, accompanied by a perfect smile. Ads for this image can be found almost everywhere we turn. For months, on one of the Employment pages of *The Toronto Star*'s Classified section there was an ad that said: "Find the person to fit the job." The person was represented as a white amorphous blotch, suggesting that "it" can take any shape, any appearance that is deemed appropriate to the job. Women's shapes and sizes (now, it seems, men's shapes and sizes as well — for certain jobs) have to fit the job description. This description does not necessarily appear in print, but it exists nonetheless in the images of advertisements, hence, in our everyday lives.

Most ads do not show women doing manual labour. Besides cleaning their houses with the wrong brand of dirt-remover, the only ads in which we see women working really hard (using their muscles) are ads for fitness programs or clubs. Here, too, almost all women are model-like; others, who are not trim and fit as a dancer, are shown in postures that provoke laughter. They are the negative prescription — we are not supposed to allow ourselves to look like them. However, their not-so-shapely bodies represent the kind of conflict we are permitted to have: conflicts about our appearance. It is a personal conflict, relegated to the level of problems — for which solutions, we are told, are widely available to everyone.

I have never seen an ad suggesting that some people, including women from any and all social classes, might be fat regardless of what and how much they have eaten, and what kind of work (or workout) they have done. It is never shown how the women who have grown fat became fat in the first place. There is never even a hint that they may have gained weight despite their own desires, on a diet that is high in carbohydrates but relatively light on the pocketbook. The diets, too, are for the wealthy. Salads, lean meats and dairy products cannot be afforded on poverty level incomes or below. Yet on page after page of women's magazines we are served up "the solution," the garden fresh vegetables with shrimp, diet supplements and pills and various spa treatments, among other miracles.

Some years after Liz stopped dancing she became a fitness club manager, where having a certain body shape and size are basic requirements for the job. To run a fitness club, a woman has to be thin *and* muscular. In addition to having to build her muscles because of the job, Liz also worked on making her body more muscular because her husband — a man she had met on one of her business trips — also encouraged Liz to do body-building. He wanted her to have a perfect body.

In the first three decades of Liz's life, then, the ideal of the attractive feminine body changed three times: first, muscular and voluptuous, then thin and lean and, later, thin and muscular. When voluptuous was "in," Liz despised herself for being flat-chested and angular. After thin became fashionable, she loved herself when she lost weight and hated herself when she gained weight. When thin and muscular were "in," she toned her muscles to fit the new image.

As one reviewer of the movie *Pumping Iron II: The Women* remarked, "The days of Twiggy are gone .... some members of the 'weaker sex' are developing their muscles and sculpting their bodies by lifting weights." Since the late 1970s, "... a woman's place seemed increasingly to be in the gym" (*The Globe and Mail* 3 May 1985, E1). In an article on women body-builders in Toronto, A. Sokol described one such woman this way:

> Valerie weighs the same 120 pounds as when she started pumping iron, but now has only 4 per cent body fat on her frame.

The average woman has about 20 % body fat, but Phillips' physique is not what you would call average.

The reason she rides the bicycle two hours a day, six days a week is not so much to develop aerobic (heart-lung) efficiency as to rid herself of fat. Her diet this week consists of 400 calories a day; a Big Mac contains about 500 calories.

Phillips knows the name and function of every muscle in her dynamic body, having studied physiology, biology and kinesiology at Seneca College as part of her coaching program. She is also a student of nutrition. (Sokol 1985, F4)

In recent ads for Super Fitness, female members are being solicited by showing pictures of women with huge, unusually developed muscles. The days of Twiggy have begun to fade, but it seems that they have merely been replaced by another craze that centres women's attention on the body as a valuable commodity. Meanwhile, ads and articles in which thinness is advocated continue to appear in the daily papers with titles such as "Losing Weight Without Lifting a Finger." This article opens with a quotation that is an ad for the new method of weight reduction, using computer-controlled electric stimulation:

> I hate exercising. I'm busy. I'm lazy. This is the lazy woman's way to do it. It beats all the others. I wanted to lose weight and I did — 17 pounds. (Irene Dale, children's clothing manufacturer) (*The Toronto Star* 25 Jan. 1985, C1)

Thin is still definitely "in," as an advertisement in a December 13, 1987 issue of *The New York Times Magazine* amply illustrates. On a full-page picture a very slim model, "Kim Cooper — 79% fat free," is shown working out with weights. The caption is: "There is more fat on her than on our salami." And then the statistics: "Even a woman in great shape is, on average, 21% fat National salami is only 17% fat." We are then advised that this "good, old fashioned, 100% beef, kosher salami" makes a nutritional, low-fat lunch. That's what Kim eats when she feels like having a "great tasting" lunch. The ad closes with the logo of Hebrew National salami and these words: "You Should Be So Lean" (p. 59).

Fitness has also been a synonym for youth. In the *City Dweller* (Toronto), there is an ad for The Beverly Hills Face Clinic. Underneath the photo of a woman said to be 50 years old, we read: "Face Fitness" (in large, bold print). "Look 10 years younger with the Fabulous Face Firming Facial. Smoothes lines, puffiness, and saggy skin. To keep your skin looking beautiful, phone today for an appointment" (March-April 1985, 5). In this example, as in so many others, "fitness" is the catchword; it camouflages as the elixir for eternal youth that advertisers have been selling women for a long, long time. And like all other ads, it betrays a hatred of women by incessantly telling them that they are no good as they are.

Even a cursory look at popular media materials suggests that fitness is not only equated with youth but with health as well. We are now offered Total Fitness packages: fitness, health and nutrition all in one deal. Although choice in exercise and diet is a favourite word in the description of such packages, what constitute proper diet and exercise are in fact rigidly defined. Hiking, walking, bicycling or swimming — for the enjoyment of these activities, primarily for pleasure — are not in the repertoire of choices. The hazards of the recommended and prescribed activities — such as knee and back injuries related to running on concrete and aerobics — are almost never discussed. Fitness and health are presented entirely as individual responsibilities. Work-related dangers, poverty and environmental pollution are not part of the discourse on fitness and health. The image of the healthy body that has been created is a well-tanned woman or man who works out regularly (does aerobic exercises, runs or jogs and or lifts weights), eats foods that have been deemed healthy and has a body that is both thin and muscular. Fitness and health, as presented in the popular media have little — if anything — to do with a person's well-being. Instead, they are descriptions of a person's appearance, of the degree to which she conforms to a certain culturally constructed and endorsed image of acceptable looks.

Such a casting of fitness and health is an example of the operation Berger and Luckmann call "nihilation" (1967, 59-160). In this, the past is radically reformulated by the repudiation of alternative realities. The past is reconstructed in a manner that invalidates all interpretations that are inconsistent with the presently claimed view of reality. To illustrate: when I recently met an acquaintance who appeared to have lost a great deal of weight and I asked her how it happened, she said that she wanted to be slimmer and healthier; she realized she had not taken care of herself before — she had not exercised and paid attention to her diet, and now she felt much better. With this response she negated the plausible interpretation that she had been healthy and fit, although in a different sense, before she lost weight. Another example of nihilation is Jane Fonda's "realization" that her life was really important to her and "... the choice was between being a good mother and wife and being a bulimic" (Janos 1985, 170).

Like Jane Fonda, who has both shaped and been shaped by the currently popular view of fitness and health, many other actresses have also published books on beauty, fitness and health. Several of them are women in their forties and fifties who may not have as many opportunities to act on screen and stage as they once did and have jumped on the fitness bandwagon. I was leafing through Sophia Loren's book, *Women and Beauty*, and found to my dismay the once-celebrated beauty heavily made-up and outfitted in a white track suit bearing the letters "U." (in blue) "S." (in white) "A." (in red) and the five interlocking rings, the symbol of the olympic games. Loren was demonstrating the head roll, toe touch, arm reach and circles, leg stretch and so on. The photos that take up most of the pages of this book are from either a by-gone era (her movies from decades ago) or portray a very wealthy and attractive woman. This book presents an ideal of beauty that is accessible to very few women in this world, because it requires a level of disposable income the overwhelming majority of women do not have. By implication, women who do not approximate Loren's appearance are not attractive, beautiful or fit.

"Fitness," "health" and slimness are multibillion-dollar businesses. Just how much profit is made off the sweat and pain of women (and, increasingly men) no one seems to know exactly. But Lean Cuisine reported a tenfold increase in sales from 1982 to 1987; sugar companies and NutraSweet are fighting over market share, as are producers and packagers of chicken and red meat (Johnson 1987). Since red meat has been given a bad name, chicken consumption increased by fifty percent in a decade. (Incidentally, I have noticed that chickens have grown fatter and thicker-skinned than ever.) The ads for NutraSweet and chicken have been less than honest, to say the least. "The industries that thrive because of weight loss ... feed, intentionally or otherwise, on misinformation and fear" — mostly fear of fat (Johnson 1987, 72). People who join weight-loss programs spend about a thousand dollars just on the programs themselves, and dietary supplements and other related expenses are not included in this figure.

We also know that two or three new diet books are published every year — even though there is not much that is really new about dieting. The release of these new books is timed for after the New Year — the "fat season." *The Complete Scarsdale Medical Diet* sold eight million soft cover and one million hard cover copies by 1984; *The Pritikin Permanent Weight-Loss Manual* sold three million copies by the same year (Slopen 1984). Before the boom of the video business, when Jane Fonda workout tapes could be brought in large numbers into our homes, Fonda received three million dollars in royalties a year. Now there are also audio tapes we can listen to as we drive or ride to work, advising us about fitness, health, slimness and nutrition. There are running (and, more recently, walking) shoes for every type of terrain and activity, as well as workout clothes that come with matching accessories in fashion colours and more.

With all the aids, remedies and package deals now available, women are enticed with increasing force to view themselves externally, not unlike the way we look at commodities to purchase. In the last interview, Liz said, "I feel men have treated me as a commodity." Men have related to her as a thing to look at, show off, use — and abuse — as they wished. And although Liz understood that men have treated her as a commodity, this understanding has not dispelled her concern with wanting to be attractive. She has continued to be afraid of gaining more than a couple of pounds. Now divorced, Liz is aware that she is popular with men because she is slim and attractive. She wants to continue working and be married again, and a thin and attractive body is a prerequisite for both. She does not like being alone. My sense is that, beside yearning for companionship, love and affection, Liz also wants to be married because the pressure on women to be married continues to be paramount. In recent years, the desirability of monogamous heterosexual relationships in marriage has been reinforced by the threat of AIDS. Also, images of the single woman continue to be largely negative. A single woman is thought of as a lonely woman. This image implies that something is wrong with her, that she has failed to attract and keep a man. She is often pitied for not having a man's protection or feared and despised if she has or is suspected of having relationships with other women. In our society, women are not supposed to lavish their care and affection on other women.

During her "rocky marriage," while all her "problems got worse" — Liz "binged and purged worse than ever," while supporting her husband and his children from an earlier relationship and taking primary responsibility for the entire family. Liz also managed to study and obtained a professional degree. Over the past few years, she has pursued a career. She often spends twelve or more hours a day at work — her job is very demanding, but she also works long days because she prefers not to spend the evenings alone at home. Since her divorce, she has tried to make new friends. If possible, she'd like to have children of her own. It is only recently that she has begun to "discover women as friends," without feeling competitive or jealous of them as before. She has been less concerned about her weight than just a few years ago, but still it is very important to her to remain slim.

Liz knows that when she goes home to her empty apartment is the time that she most wants to binge. She tries to have something to do in the evening — drop into a bar after work for a glass of wine or go to a fitness club — to stay away from food. Katrina usually binged on weekends, and Simone — for many years — binged almost any time when she was alone at home. Liz clearly recognized a pattern for binging: whenever her life seemed unfulfilled, whenever nothing interesting or rewarding was happening, she wanted food.

Similar to Simone, when Liz was showing me pictures of herself, her family and friends, she spoke in a detached voice, as if she were not talking about herself at all. The only time I heard a sparkle in her voice was when she showed a couple of baby pictures of "daddy's little girl" — Liz when she was loved, admired and accepted without having to do anything except, perhaps, smile at daddy. When she spoke of other women in the pictures, she usually introduced them with a brief description of their appearance, which always included some statement about their weight.

This is, in a nutshell, Liz's life story. Although Liz was well-versed in the "dos" and "do nots" of ladylike appearance and manners, she felt acutely aware of not being perfect, not measuring up. In the same way as Katrina and Simone, she always found something wrong with herself. If she was thin, then her nose was too big, or her face still looked childish because it was round and she had dimples or something else was wrong; she could never be pretty enough. Despite the fact that Liz has come to see herself as attractive in a certain way and fashionably thin, when she goes to a party and a man does not talk to her, her first thought still is: "It's because I'm not good looking enough."

CHAPTER FOUR

VARIATIONS ON
A THEME

JUDITH WAS FAT BY age four. She described her life as "miserable" before she started school. Children teased her — "fatty, fatty, two-by-four, can't get through the bathroom door." Although she had a few friends, she was not very comfortable with them. She often played alone at home, in a playroom her parents set up for her.

When she was born, her mother was in her mid-forties. The youngest of her three brothers and sisters was ten years old. The family lived on the coast in low-income housing. Judith's father was a blue-collar worker. Her mother worked part-time in a store when Judith's father was laid off. The parents purchased a house when Judith was a child, and later, when they retired, they sold the house and moved to a condominium.

The family took vacations together every year, visiting with a relative at a nearby resort place. Judith enjoyed those times, the attention she received from her aunt, the swimming and horseback riding. She went camping with the brownies and guides she had joined. She liked being outdoors and enjoyed reading about animals and adventures.

Judith, much like Simone, was aware by the time she reached school age that her body looked different from that of other children. She hated herself for being fat. She had trouble with gym classes; she thought she could not do sports. She was frustrated by and ashamed of her body; it limited and sometimes prevented her from taking part in activities with other children.

Judith was a hard-working student, getting through school with "A"s. But she felt very insecure. As she got older, she was teased less for her weight and more for her "brains." She became very active at school, taking on leadership and organizational responsibilities. She continued her involvement with the guides and, later, the rangers, going camping and earning badges.

By grade eight, Judith had gained a considerable amount of weight. Her family ate balanced meals, and not to excess, yet they all were overweight. At age fourteen Judith decided to lose weight. She managed to do so, by being very active, sleeping little, cutting back severely on portions and eating mainly low-calorie foods.

For grade twelve, Judith left her small Catholic school and went to a public high school. By then she had been dieting on and off for three years. The new and bigger school made it even more important to be slim, she said, because it was a chance to meet new people. She was afraid that, if she was not thinner, she would be rejected; she would have no dates; she would have no friends; she would not be popular. When she lost about thirty pounds, she "enjoyed" the way she looked "much more" and "felt much more at ease with males."

She was not, however, popular with boys. She went out with one boy at age fifteen, and later, when she was at university, she dated another one for a few months. She began to be more involved with the youth group of the church, doing a lot of volunteer work.

Judith, much like Simone, hated herself and felt miserable as a child for being fat. Even when she lost over twenty percent of her body weight, "the horrible feelings never left. I still thought I was not thin enough; I was just better," said Judith. Elaborating on her long-standing desire to have "no extra fat" on her body, she stated, "I'd like to be as good as possible." For all the women studied, being fat was clearly being "bad." Describing how they felt about themselves when they were not thin (or not as thin as they thought they should be), they used words such as "disgusting," "miserable," "piggish," "hateful," "ugly." Being thin, on the other hand, meant being "good" — "the best I can be," "lovable" and "deserving of respect."

Judith's vision of her future was that of a lay apostle, a single woman committed to teaching and living Christian values. She wanted to go on to university, to get a degree in social science. Ultimately, she wanted a Ph.D. After earning her B.A., Judith started to work and lived alone for a few years. She met someone who wanted to marry her. Although Judith was ambivalent at first — she had not planned to get married — she eventually agreed because, as she described it, she was feeling "very needy [lonely] at the time."

In the first year of their marriage, just before their daughter was born, Judith and her husband left the coast and moved to a small town. Living in a new environment, with a new marriage and a new baby, Judith felt frustrated, isolated and lonely much of the time. While sitting up with the baby many nights and, alternately, trying to get her to sleep, she felt there was nothing in her life that she really enjoyed; there was not a thing just for her. During this period, Judith started to eat more. She nibbled throughout the day and kept gaining weight, until she finally found a job in the nearby city. Once she was working in a paid job, she ate less and slowly began to lose weight.

Judith then decided to concentrate on losing weight; she made a point of exercising more, and followed the Scarsdale diet. She was "doing well" on her diet until she was promoted to a high pressure position that required her to return to school for further studies. Whenever pressure built up, Judith said, she turned to food — for comfort and because she liked eating:

> So I started to eat too much again; there was a lot of tension....
> And this summer I decided, "this is crazy. If I don't do something

I'll just keep going up." And I wanted to do something. I have joined a fitness centre over at work ... with the hope that it would help. Well, it didn't. In fact, I kept gaining weight. For me, I have to diet as well as exercise. So I realized I'd just have to cut way back, and so I have.

I felt at that point I could not do it on my own. I needed some help.... It's about despair. It's about feeling incapable. At that point it was long since I'd been able to see tangible results or control my eating.

Judith had tried various crash diets, gone to Weight Watchers and diet workshops before. This time, she said, she wanted something with "more structure," that is, with more frequent contact. She went to a weight-loss clinic, even though she thought it was "frivolous to spend all that money" on herself. But it was, as she said, about despair, and she spent over three-hundred dollars on the program.

When Judith and Simone were losing weight, people began to comment on how wonderfully they looked as they became slimmer. It was after hearing such comments that they stopped trying to ignore their bodies and divert attention from how they looked as they had previously. As the "slimmest and best me" seemed to become a possibility, Simone's and Judith's concern with their bodies and appearance became more explicit. Fascination combined with a compelling sense of necessity in the relentless pursuit of the "ideal body for me." Judith said that she was really curious about what "it" (her thinner body) would look like. For Simone, becoming as thin as possible was connected with an ethereal fantasy, with a transformation of becoming a princess. Both Judith and Simone felt that they absolutely had to be thin. Their worth, their future, their entire existence seemed to depend on it.

Judith believed that it is through being thin, by exercising self-control in our eating — that we can demonstrate to others our psychological health. She found that looking healthy is a requirement for being acceptable, respectable and worthy of being (or having been) offered a job. She explained this point as follows:

> In a sense, it is our physical appearance that others see first. For me, in my job, people come in to see me, and they get an immediate impression. I don't want my body to interfere with what I can offer.... And I don't want my mental state [preoccupation with food and dieting] to interfere either.

Judith's comments about having to be thin are all the more noteworthy because she is not working in a job where — at least I thought — being fashionably thin would matter very much. She is a public-service employee. Initially, I was very surprised to learn that a woman, especially a married woman, employed in this sector would have to be so concerned about how thin she was. As I was listening to Judith, I began to understand that women pursue thinness not only to attract and keep a man, but also to attract and keep a job. Their advancement in the job, the size of their pay cheques, their livelihood, depends on how closely they approximate to the current ideal of feminine appearance. But, beyond this necessity for a living wage, how they are treated by fellow workers, superiors and their clients in daily interactions also hinges on their size and shape, as Judith suggested.

I was also surprised to learn that Judith believed that, if she achieved and maintained a certain weight, she would no longer be concerned with food and dieting. Her mental state would improve. I was caught off guard by her statement. I had just spent four months working with women who had dieted, starved themselves, binged and purged. I had seen how preoccupied they were with their weight and food at 90, 80, 70 pounds and less. If anything, they thought more about what they ate and how the food made them look the more weight they lost. They believed that the only thing that prevented them from being happy was the "extra" weight on their bodies. Alarmed by Judith's anticipation of improved mental state with weight loss, I started to plead with her. I told her about the women with whom I had worked. I wanted her to stop dieting before it was too late. I wanted her to stop worrying about what the scale or the mirror showed. To improve our lives as women, it is not our shape and size that have to be altered. As I talked, I had a sinking feeling that my plea went against the tide; it was too little and perhaps too late to counter the messages flooding us daily.

As Judith's experiences demonstrate, to be considered healthy or fit in our society, one must be thin. A fat woman is regarded as lacking self-control. People say, she must have grown fat because she has psychological problems. Here is how Judith explained this point:

> Being overweight is often taken as a lack of control. "Well, gee, that person sure has a problem!" It's how I think about people who are largely overweight.... Very critically. You know, I mean, it's obvious, because there is not a medical problem in the majority of situations, they just eat too much.

There may be no medical problems; we just don't all come in the same shape and size. Obvious, though, as this observation is, we are urged to act as if there was only one mold, one norm, from which we deviate *and we should not*. Women are led to believe that if only they stopped eating and lost weight, they would be perfect; they could look like any of the models; they could "instantly become like one of them," as Simone said.

Nearly all the successful women — women who are presented as models for us — are tall, thin, young and healthy looking (as well as dressed in elegant and expensive clothes). After years of struggle trying to be like one of these ideals, Simone remarked that she could never be "an amazon." Since she was short, the only thing she could change was her weight. Judith, using almost the same words as Simone, said she could try to make herself thin and healthy looking, but not tall:

> Of course, I'll never look like the ideal North American perfect figure ... [which is] about 5'5" and fairly hourglass proportioned. You go in at the waist, the hips are not too big, and the breasts are adequate, fairly balanced top and bottom.... There is nothing I can

do about my height, obviously, *but there is something I can do about my weight*. It's something that's within a person's control to a certain extent, I think to a large extent, but I may find I'm wrong.

Indeed, there is a lot some women can do about their weight. They can lose ten, fifty, some even a hundred or more pounds — and, within a year, 95 percent of the dieters put back the weight they lost and some more. Canadians spend on average about $1,000 before they give up on weight-loss programs. Over three-fourths of women believe they are too fat, and I have never met a woman who was honestly satisfied with her body shape and size.

Why is it that women are never satisfied with their bodies? Why is it that even the models upheld as our ideals live on grapefruit and salads and an occasional half sandwich? If we follow Marian Lowe's argument, it is because the differences between women's and men's bodies have been emphasized and exaggerated. "In part, we literally may be shaped by our social roles," rather than by our biology, as (socio-) biological determinist theorists would have us believe (Lowe 1982, 91). When women are encouraged to be physically more active, they become more similar to men, in terms of strength, than to other women. Her review of research on sex differences in strength, physical and intellectual performance, height and various other characteristics typically attributed to innate biological-sexual differences suggests that sex differences should be explained in sociocultural terms. Understood in such terms, innate biology cannot be isolated as an independent realm, and it in no way accounts for women's femininity.

Unlike Lowe, Rolland Barthes (1982) argues that today men's and women's clothes, hence their bodies, are more similar than in previous eras, that sexual differences are less pronounced. Further, as the body is liberated from clothing and nudity is permitted to appear, the body liberates itself. It seems to me that, although in some cases the dress codes are less sex-specific than in the past and at times we cover less of the body than we used to, the body's liberation may be more apparent than real. We may be projecting a freer body image ("we" meaning people of relative wealth in the Western world), and women's less restrictive clothing has facilitated their participation in activities that were previously taboo for them. Nonetheless, women's and men's bodies continue to be both differentiated and restricted.

Despite the apparent similarities in men's and women's clothing and bodies, the differences continue to be emphasized. New versions of femininity have been produced on a mass-scale; the recent phenomenon of the relentless pursuit of thinness is a good example of this trend. "The tyranny of slenderness" forces women into seeking to achieve a certain body shape and marginalizes those women whose shape and size deviates from this prescription (Chernin 1981). The differences that exist among women's bodies are forced to diminish; women are urged incessantly to reduce — to be like the models of femininity presented to them.

Forcing women's bodies into one mold perpetuates the sexual differentiation between women and men. The ways in which women's bodies are like men's remains, to a large degree, hidden. The differences between men's and women's bodies continue to be produced, although the shape that is dictated for women's bodies has changed.

Yet, Barthes is also right. There is a new dictum of conformity to uniformity: the phenomenon of ageism or "young racism." The diminished differentiation between women and men may relate more to the privileged status accorded to youth than to decreasing sexual differentiation *per se*. Women and men are more similar in so far as they must project a youthful image, of which thinness is one component.

Youth is a symbol of immortality, and capitalism needs for its existence consumers who do not think of the finiteness of their lives and keep consuming. A special anniversary issue of *Omni* magazine (Oct. 1986) is devoted exclusively to "longevity." The cover page announces reports on "youth pills, laser face-lifts, born-again genes, souls on ice, artificial skin, surrogate brains and much, much more!" *Omni*'s president Kathy Keeton, herself an advertisement for youth and wealth, suggests that instead of spending on health care for the aged, the government should fund longevity research to find a "cure for the disease called old age." She ends on what we are to read as an optimistic note: "The news from today's biochemists, plastic surgeons, and geron-tologists is that you *can* stretch out those years of youth. *Longevity* will tell you how. The right to a long and healthy life should be available to all people; it should be as fundamental as the right to free speech" (p. 6).

Today's body is not only a weightless body (Schwartz 1986), it is also an eternally youthful, forever healthy body. Judith said that, even if she did not need to be thin in order to be "presentable" at work, she would still try to lose weight "to be as thin as possible" — for health reasons:

> I'd try to be healthy, in a proactive and retroactive sense. Proactive — it is good to be at moderate weight; it's better for your heart and bones. Retroactive — in the sense of being free from back aches, which I have had, and being free of sore knees, like when I first joined the fitness club at work jumping around hurt my knees.

In order to improve one's health, it is important to become slim — so Judith and all of us have been told. This includes both physical health in the proactive and retroactive sense, and mental health, as Judith explained. And, she added, although a woman should avoid aiming for the "extreme" — having a skeleton-like body — she should make sure not to eat more than her body requires. This means that a woman must make sure that "no extra fat" clings to her body frame, because it does not "look good" and, as we have often heard, can present a health hazard.

Youth, health and thinness are intertwined in women's lives through the popular media in a capitalist political-economic system. In a book entitled *Never Satisfied*, Schwartz (1986) demonstrates that world food production, the crisis of capitalism and the production of desire are interrelated and, together, produce the contemporary Western body ideals that can never be reached. He suggests that, in an expanding capitalist world, people are never permitted to be fully satisfied; confusion of hunger and appetite is encouraged. In Schwartz's analysis, the seemingly personal dilemma of millions of women concerning their body shape and size emerges as a genuine political-economic issue.

Similarly to Schwartz, Silverstein (1984) analyzes the current obsession with thinness in terms of the needs of capitalism. He places the issue of eating disorders squarely into a socio-economic context and blames the food industry under capitalism for the co-existence of overeating, malnutrition and the weight-obsession of North Americans. For political-economic reasons, he argues, women have been explicitly targeted to be particularly obsessed with their bodies.

What has it taken for Judith, Liz, Simone and the other women to lose those pounds? What struggles have they gone through? Although she has not binged and purged like Simone, Judith has anxiously lived the conflict between wanting to eat and wanting to be slim:

> There is a basic struggle going on. I want food now. I like food. I like the taste; it makes me feel better. And the opposing thing is, well, it'll make me feel fatter. I feel satisfied, relieved, comforted by eating something.

When she comforts herself with food, she almost immediately says, "Ah, shit! Here I go again!" And, "Well, what's the use. I have ruined it tonight!" At this point, she goes on to eat some more — "automatically and quickly" — for comfort. Then she worries about what the scale will show the following day and how other people will judge her for her fatness as representing her lack of self-control. Furthermore, Judith knows that her husband appreciates her more when she is thin. He would like to have "romantic evenings" with his wife, enjoying a good bottle of wine with their meal. But if Judith wants to be more appreciated by him, she has to diet, which means no wine with her dinner and saying "no" to most of the food on the menu. She is caught between wanting the satisfaction of eating and her husband's appreciation for a thin body. Satisfaction evades her if she eats, and it evades her if she does not.

Like all the other interviewed women, Judith learned that a woman must always watch her figure and must take care not to gain any weight even if it means dieting every day of her life. Watching one's figure, however, is deceptive. As Judith found, she appeared fat to herself unless she was losing weight. And losing weight is rewarded by compliments from strangers and acquaintances. A husband also appreciates his wife more if she is thin, though Judith added that she (he?) wished her breasts would remain the "the right size" as she kept losing weight.

When Judith was gaining weight, she began to feel panicky. The exercise program she joined at work did not prevent the weight gain. That's why she decided that she had to seek help — she did not think she could lose weight alone. She went to a weight-loss clinic and over a three-month period lost nearly thirty pounds. She was "happy with the result," as was her husband. But shortly after school started again, with the pressures on Judith increasing — to manage a demanding job, studies and a family — her weight again started to increase. In the context of talking about what it was like for her to look at herself naked in the mirror Judith said:

> I find it hard, right now, to look at myself naked. I don't like what I see. Most of the time I avert my eyes.... There is too much here [she points at her stomach]; it sticks out too far. And before it was like there's too much here [she points at her breasts] and here [her thighs]. I find it very curious — I have noticed it not long ago — that unless I see myself going down I see myself as fat.... I thought this is ridiculous. Here I am, maybe twenty-eight pounds less than a few months ago, and I see myself as fat. This is crazy.

Judith could not have weighed more than 115-20 pounds at the time when she felt it was "crazy" to see herself as fat because she had just lost 28 pounds. When I heard this, Simone's words came to mind: "I don't want to go on a diet, but I am not sure except that I feel fat. I felt fat at 94 pounds, so how good is my judgement?"

I wanted to interview Judith for this study because based on what I had known about her, her practices around eating and dieting did not seem as extreme as any of the other women's. She could not be considered by any criteria either anorexic or bulimic. Along the "eating arc" (Squire 1984, 7), she would be placed as a "chronic dieter" (ibid., 7). Like hundreds of thousands of weight-conscious women, she has tried fad diets and weight-loss programs, but she has not binged and purged, nor has her weight dropped to a dangerously low level. Her adult weight has fluctuated by twenty-five to thirty pounds (not counting pregnancy), and she has struggled to keep it in the range life-insurance charts consider normal for her height and body frame.

I wanted to interview a woman whose practices are a fairly typical example of a great number of women's efforts to diet in our society today. Likely due to my training in psychopathology, I was not prepared for the similarities between some of Judith's statements and those of anorexic and bulimic women. I thought that the experiences and practices of women who simply diet are radically different from the experiences and practices of women hospitalized with eating disorders. I could not have been more wrong.

The most striking example of this similarity for me was when Judith said that she wanted to be "as thin as possible," she wanted "no extra fat," and she was prepared to do whatever was necessary to become as thin as she could be. These statements are identical with those made by women hospitalized for anorexia nervosa. When Judith described her daily struggles around food, her experiences also showed a frightful resemblance to the experiences of women with eating disorders. Food and dieting have occupied a major place in her life; for some periods they were her main concern. Where do we draw the lines, then? On what basis can we ever say, "She is only dieting, but this other woman is anorexic"? In the discourse of thinness, health does not refer to everyone having a well-balanced diet, adequate housing in an ecologically sound environment, sufficient work and recreational opportunities and freedom from habits that are damaging to oneself and others. Described in this manner, health — as well as our preoccupation with building a "better" body — would be immediately recognized as essentially a social, political, economic and educational issue. Instead, health is presented to us as a matter of life-style choice that each of us individually can and should make:

> In the narcissistic 1980s, physical perfection — from head to toe — is the new status symbol. According to the experts, it's also a reflection of our society's search for control. We may not be able to stop the arms race, get a raise or even get a job. But we can build a better body.
> *"It is something that people can do for themselves."* (*The Toronto Star* 21 April 1984, M1)

The quest for "physical perfection" may very well be a manifestation of our search for control when we feel powerless to tackle the burning issues in our immediate life situations, in our society and in the world. Simone and other anorexic women come to mind who spoke of having control over nothing save their own bodies. Beyond being a manifestation of our search for control, however, the now pervasive preoccupation with perfecting the body is a *substitute* for activities that may help transform our life situations. I recently heard of a couple with serious financial and other troubles in their relationship whose solution was literally to get in shape. Trimming waist lines and developing muscles was their seemingly personal solution to real conflict and contradictions in their — and our — lives. Acting as if public troubles could be resolved at a personal level — by body shaping — strikes me as participating willingly in our own exploitation and oppression.

I do not mean to blame people as individuals for such pseudosolutions for life crises and crises on a global scale. But, in contemporary liberal individualism, our knowledge is organized as isolated persons working hard each on our own, and we do think we should take care of ourselves. The suggested solution to overcome conflicts and contradictions in our lives is to improve our self-concept. Health is now equated with positive self-concept or, as fitness-guru Jane Fonda put it, with liking ourselves. Responding to accusations that she had been advocating exercise to make women thinner, Fonda said that the purpose of exercise is to become healthier "so that people can like themselves more" (*Life in the Fat Lane*, CBS TV, 3 June 1987). This statement contains a grain of truth — in our society at present it is very difficult for women to like themselves if they don't conform to the current body ideal. But it tells us nothing about why most women cannot like themselves if they are not thinner, healthier or whatever other term is to be associated with exercise. And, regardless of Fonda's defence, the message of the CBS program to women was, "eat less, exercise more, and do it forever." It all seems so simple. It's all really up to you — just make a habit of cutting down on food and working up a sweat regularly.

Exercising — where else but in a fitness club? — can do even more than help us get in shape, become healthier and develop a positive self-concept. The health and fitness clubs have been presented as a unique site of romance. M. Horton, in an article in *Slimmer* magazine, calls them "a place for singles to meet." It is such a wonderful place for romance because here the two "start out with so much in common." The prospective partners share a "dedication to good health" and an "interest in working out." Since "... they are keeping their health longer ... [they] have more time to spend with one another" (Horton 1985, 32). Such superficial similarities in people's life-styles bring and bind them together in work, entertainment and marriage. Here we observe a new brand of the commodification of romance and the production of interpersonal relationships in the careful process of packaging. Everything has been scrutinized and calculated, our habits, our life expectancy and even the length of the marriage singles pursuing health-club romances can expect.

In our present political-economic structure, "Everybody is to everybody else a commodity" (Fromm 1955, 126). Human beings' worth is also defined in terms of their health as a commodity. The healthier the workers are, the less days they miss. According to 1979 estimates, absenteeism cost Canada $4.9 billion and OHIP (Ontario Health Insurance Plan) could save over $30 million yearly if Ontarians improved their fitness level (*Scotton* 1984, M1, M9). It is to increase the company's profits that Ontario Hydro, for instance, tried to "get people hooked on the idea of getting fit." After an initial "fitness motivation" course Hydro sought to keep its workers hooked by negotiating lower rates for its employees with health clubs. The company gave the initial impetus to its workers to jump on the fitness bandwagon, and peer pressure did the rest — as one employee said, "... you feel you have to be there" (ibid.) And you have to pay up — even if at discount rates.

Conforming to the fit image has become one facet of packaging our appearance and making ourselves saleable. In our "receptive orientation" we rush around "to have something new all the time, to live with a continuously open mouth, as it were" (Fromm 1955, 124). We take in leisure time, movies, trips, spectator sports, restaurants and fitness, and we purchase the necessary accessories for these activities. But, in all these activities, people remain alienated consumers who are never satisfied, never full. People have been led to seek, to have experiences (photographable moments, really) as substitutes for experiences they perhaps could have had but did not have. We do not consume real and concrete things, we drink labels and eat a fantasy.

By popping [frozen Lean Cuisine] dinners into the microwave oven for seven minutes ... Canada's calorie counter culture can play out a nightly fantasy of obtaining the perfect body while consuming the perfect meal. (Johnson 1987, 68)

Or we can fantasize about being Monika Schnarre, the latest Canadian teenage super model earning $3,000 a day for having her picture taken (*Maclean's* 13 April 1987, 36). With the fantasies offered by Lean Cuisine and weight-management groups, we enter into the impersonal market of commodities. This market, controlled by the interests of capital towards ever-increasing profits, is a necessary precondition of the objectification and feminization of women's bodies.

In our society today, women are bound together by their instruction in the lessons of femininity. All of the women studied knew exactly how many calories it takes to lose a pound, what activities burn up the most calories and even what the fat to muscle ratio of a female body "should" be. They obtained this information from a variety of sources. Most women's magazines are notorious for publishing a host of such facts in every issue. Experts in so-called health and fitness clubs and in weight-loss clinics are another source of this type of information. Most bookstores in North America have a large health section filled with books on how to diet. During a stroll down the street, in a shopping mall and even in the hallways of our schools and universities, we encounter people wearing buttons that say, "Lose weight now, ask me how." Even at work we can find, as I have for years now, memos asking us to join "Weight Watchers at Work." These memos "proudly announce" the total amount of weight that members in the previous group lost together — as if this was the greatest achievement of working women.

But we do not even have to step outside our home to get the message that if we have not yet learned about how to diet and shape up it is time that we do. Television is, of course, a constant reminder and relentless teacher about the "ins" and "outs" of dieting. It is nearly impossible to watch television without being exposed to ads for low-calorie drinks and foods. Pamphlets dropped into our mailboxes and unsolicited telephone messages ensure that we do not forget the importance of being thin. As I was working on this research one day, the phone rang and I heard the following words:

> This is Jennifer speaking to you through a computer. You may be interested to learn that now you can lose up to thirty pounds in a month without exercise, expensive diet aids or surgeries. If you'd like more information about this new program, please leave your name and phone number after the tone.

Unfortunately, I lost my cool, and instead of leaving my name and phone number to learn more about this program, I yelled some four-letter words and banged the phone down. I was upset at this intrusion in my life, at the stream of messages to lose weight that — it seemed — I could not escape.

The so-called eating disorders cannot be grasped in isolation from the issues of objectification and feminization of women's bodies. There is no technical solution, no purely medical cure for anorexia nervosa, bulimia or obesity, just as there was no cure for hysteria, and there is likely to be none (of the technical-medical variety) for other sociocultural epidemics (Bruch 1979) yet to come. More than the death rates of anorexia nervosa, bulimia and simply dieting are frightening; what they bear witness to — the inhumanity of life under the oppressive regimes of plenty — is equally threatening.

How we feel about our bodies has to be viewed both in relation to the body as project, conditioned by circumstances and wanting to actualize certain goals, and in the broader social-historical context of the conditioning that shapes, without determining, the goal. The emptiness that women in the pursuit of thinness experience is comprehensible only within this broader conception that includes the objectifying look at the bodies of ourselves and others, as well as the objectification and exploitation of those who have not, by those who have, in a patriarchal class society.

Historically, women have not been concerned with making themselves feminine or attractive by and for themselves. Attractiveness has been most women's means of survival. When a woman is not attractive — by current white North American and Western European cultural standards — her livelihood is threatened. She is "somebody" (allowed to exist) only in relation to men. When she is not desired by men, she does not *get*, she cannot *be*, except under the harshest conditions. When many women look at themselves as objects, their look asks: "Am I desirable? Will a man want me? What kind of a man can I get? What kind of a life can I have?" Even the women considered most beautiful and often depicted as untouchable "put on a face" for men to adore — and for their own survival.

It was inconceivable to me that the way women lived in their bodies could be accounted for in terms of their "individual psychopathologies," as most of the literature does. The more I read, saw and learned about young middle-class women's lives in North America, the more it seemed to me that the women I saw in the hospital engaged in practices very similar to those of many women with whom I came into contact in my everyday life. Despite differences between how much an anorexic woman's life revolves around her diet as compared to any dieting woman I have met, I have heard both "anorexic" women and women who were "simply dieting" say: "I was happiest (most pleased with myself) when I was thinnest."

My experience of my body is quite different from the experiences of dieting women. I can describe this experience in terms of what I am able and not able to *do*. Most of my waking life I am hardly aware of my body. I wake up in the morning and go through a certain routine without paying particular attention to my body. I may ponder over what to put on if have a job interview, otherwise I don't much care about what I wear. During the day, I become aware of my body when I realize I am hungry or thirsty or I have to go to the washroom. If I go to a public washroom, and I see other women combing their hair and applying make-up, I may also glance at myself and note what I look like — nowadays mostly my greying hair, which doesn't bother me.

I may become more aware of my body if, after a day of work, I load my bags with groceries. I then wish I had a bigger and stronger body. Or, when later that night I still want to do some work, but my back is hurting, I may be annoyed with the body I have. I am pleasantly aware of my body when I take a long walk or swim or do some physical work or activity that is not part of my daily routine. I eat when I am hungry — what I have at home or can afford — and then I forget about food. My body is not the focus of my attention most of the day; it usually becomes that if my bodily experience prevents me from engaging in an activity I want to pursue.

In contrast to this description, women in the relentless pursuit of thinness struggle with how something they eat is going to make them look, not what the food they eat is going to allow them to *do*. In the practices of the relentless pursuit of thinness, the body becomes an object for showing and being looked at. It is a body on display much of the time. The body is not taken for granted in the routine of daily living and action. By dieting, starving, binging and purging a cleavage occurs between "body" and "I"; women's bodies become psychologically split, divided, dismembered — first from without, then from within.

These practices have contributed to the development of a sense of the body as an object for others that is not right in its present shape and size, as something to control and combat. For example, Judith, discussing how she got to and through the weight-loss clinic she attended, kept referring to her eating and her body as an "it" that she cannot control. It is not she who eats compulsively, but "*it* is very compulsive." She said that she ate more than her "body needed," and she described her eating after supper when she is not hungry as "it is just pigging out."

Both Simone and Judith spoke as if food was an aggressor they had to fight every hour and every day of their lives. They spoke as if food threatened to take over and destroy their lives. To protect themselves from the threat of total invasion by food, Simone and Judith have turned to experts. These experts have been more than willing to rush in with their paraphernalia to help melt away fat. The experts can help but, of course, they cannot do it for you — seems to be the motto. After they have given you all the advice it's just a matter of your willpower to carry through, isn't it? It is then up to you — to diet "sanely, sensibly ... and *forever*," as the *Cosmopolitan's Super Diets & Exercise Guide* says (Fall-Winter 1984, 100).

The women who have been interviewed for this study grew up at a period when most women in this society were permitted and even encouraged to prepare for a career of their own — a career they may or may not practice later. All of them looked toward having a university degree and all of them do. Simone's and Judith's parents told them that they could study and become "whatever they wanted to be." Liz and Katrina also earned degrees in fields in which they were interested. The notion, then, that they should entertain a field of work could be found in all the life stories. But this desire for further education and a job of their own did not counter the necessity for women to conform to idealized versions of femininity.

If women are to have the opportunity to work in jobs that may pay enough to support themselves — and sometimes their families as well — they must be attractive, that is, thin, young and healthy looking. Attractiveness alone does not, of course, guarantee such jobs. It is also important to be flawlessly well-versed in every facet of what is presented as the dominant or "in" life-style. Further, even a cursory look at popular women's magazines reveals that, if women are to be successful, they must be prepared to work very hard, on both their job and their appearance. They must be willing to put in twelve hours or more daily, and they must learn new skills, including skills in how to cope with the demands of life on the way to "the top."

Similar to the other women interviewed, Judith learned to be a dutiful daughter, competent wife, mother — a superwoman. These are some of specific values and goals Judith learned:

A proper family owns its own home and has enough money for basics. Parents should ensure that their children have fun. Parents should be warm and supportive. They do not, however, need to interact with their child in a wide range of ways.

A daughter should be honest with her parents. She must visit them often even after she no longer lives at home. She must accept her mother's criticisms. She must observe her mother's warnings. She must help out with household work and refrain from complaining.

She should also entertain herself in acceptable ways — by reading, for instance, adventure and detective stories and books on animals. Watching the soaps on television, listening to music, attending lectures, meditating and being involved in church youth groups are acceptable forms of entertainment.

Judith learned painfully our society's lessons for fat women — women must avoid by all means the horror of being fat. Fat children (girls) are teased for their shape and size. Gaining weight is a terrible experience and cause for panic. Fat is bad, it suggests that the person has no self-control. Fat people hate themselves; they have little self-confidence and self-worth. Being fat gets in the way of achieving in a career, because people are judged first by their appearance.

Fat children suffer in gym classes; they think they are unable to do sports, although they may be quite comfortable camping or playing outdoors. Fat girls are undesirable and unpopular; they are unlikely to have dates; they are lonely and isolated. To diminish the painful experience of being fat, a girl or woman may try to become very active, to work and study hard. It may become important to earn marks of distinction (badges) for being outstanding in something. Conforming to rules and trying to be the best in what she does (getting "A"s at school) may get a girl recognition and praise that she otherwise would not have (no one compliments a fat girl for her looks).

She should strive to be the perfect woman, daughter, mother and wife. She should be attractively thin, watch her weight and refrain from eating food that is fattening. It is her responsibility to provide balanced meals for herself and others. Should she gain any weight, she should start a diet immediately. She must always be calorie-conscious. She should be able to cope with any family situation, including a new child, a husband working shifts, accidents, financial difficulties, etc. Women should never complain; however, they should aspire for more in life than their parents did.

Women should also be very active — mostly in their community and church group. Being active (working hard and sleeping little) also, incidentally, helps a woman lose weight. She must make sure that she is presentable to other people; she has to have proper (attractive) appearance and manners. Yet she must not be frivolous — for instance, spend too much money or time on herself.

Women should be successful, but they should also seek help from those who are more knowledgeable if they cannot cope — from their fathers with math or from professionals with losing weight. They should also be pleased with themselves, particularly with their appearance. Exercise (joining a fitness club) is an important part of working on her appearance. Working out daily also helps a woman to stay away from food. Having to pay a substantial amount to a weight-loss clinic acts as a motivating force to stick with the diet and fitness regime that experts set out for us. With the help of experts, a woman may achieve the ideal female body. The ideal body is thin, tall and hourglass shaped. There should be no "extra fat" on the body; it should consist of bones, muscles and a protective layer of fat. It is desirable to aim for a body much like that of models in advertising and stars on television. Unless women are thin, they cannot be pleased with themselves. Women should be successful with men. They must, however, avoid heavy petting, make sure they do not get pregnant, and that they are informed about the facts of life. They should be self-reliant and able to protect themselves.

Despite the many similarities in the values, norms, ideals and aspirations, there are also important differences between Judith's and the other women's lives. The most obvious one is that she has not used the more extreme means of weight control. Why? What kept her from binging and purging, for example, when she, too, must have gone hungry on her diets; when she also has been steeped in the messages to keep consuming? How is it that she stopped dieting at a low but still relatively safe weight? To repeat, after the mainstream psychiatric literature, that Judith must have had a stronger personality or that she did not think dichotomously would not even begin to answer these questions. Looking at how her immediate life situation differed from that of the other women's may, however, provide us with some clues.

Judith's involvement with groups, girls guides and church groups later on, have offered her a set of activities, interests and concerns that were an alternative to focusing almost exclusively on her appearance. She had ties to aspects of living through these involvements in groups that took her outside of herself, metaphorically speaking. From an early age, there were opportunities for Judith to develop and use a number of skills that were not related so intimately to being an attractive woman by currently popular standards. One way to depict the difference between Judith and the other women is that the main basis for existence for the latter was "having," whereas, for Judith, "doing" has become and remained her dominant mode of being. What she was able to do mattered most, not what she could have. Judith, it seems, has not shared the fantasies of romance and romantic happiness the same way as the other women did. She has lived toward more clearly defined and immediate goals, and these were also goals that she knew how to realize. Yet, living toward an alternative set of goals did not offer complete protection from having major concerns about appearance — the concerns which Judith has shared with the other interviewed women, although apparently to a lesser degree.

Judith, like Simone, was a fat child who was teased and ostracized from peer groups. Since her high-school years, Judith has attempted, time and again, to lose weight and thus make herself acceptable, respectable and avoid the punitive consequences of being fat. In her various struggles, again like Simone, she sought the help of experts to lose weight. She spoke in terms similar to Simone about her struggles with food and dieting. Judith, like Simone, seems to have been prepared to do whatever is required to become and stay as slender as she possibly can be. Judith, although she was not as obese as Simone during her childhood and has not dieted as severely, felt discriminated against, excluded from a range of activities and humiliated much of the time. The teasing and public humiliation stopped as she was growing up, but the "absence of comments" — "no one telling you how nice you looked" — did not cease. Judith's husband would say, "I love you anyway, it [your not being thin] does not matter to me." Still, Judith felt, he appreciated her much more when she lost weight. She thought other people felt the same way, for it was only when she lost weight that they started to comment on her appearance.

Judith, as we have seen, ate out of frustration, out of having nothing in her life that she liked. Katrina ate and gained weight when she began to lose hope for the "happy ever after." She ate out of rage. As I was listening to women talk about compulsive eating and binging, I thought of it as a desperate attempt to fill a void, the emptiness left after experiences of disappointment, rejection, failure. Binging offers a temporary escape from the world, a world that is experienced as utterly painful. Being fat is so unacceptable for women in this society that a fat woman can live her life as if it were not truly her own life. Her life could only start when she was no longer fat. With her face buried behind a mountain of food she can forget about the world, the pain and emptiness. She can feel full, satisfied — for the moment.

Judith has been concerned about being preoccupied with food much of the time. She has been driven by "curiosity" about what she would look like if she were as thin as possible. She also hopes that then she would stop worrying about what and how much she eats — "whether tomorrow the scale is going to be up." She thinks that if she can lose enough weight (not have any "extra fat" on her body) and keep it off, her preoccupation with food will disappear. She said that she is prepared to spend the rest of her life dieting rigidly to avoid getting fat again. As we have seen, Judith knows that it is important to be as thin as possible for "health" reasons and because people are judged by their appearance.

> The direction I have decided to take is that ... the way to get rid of all that is to get slim and stay there. Probably — realistically — it would be a struggle every day of my life.

CHAPTER FIVE

OUT OF ENTRAPMENT

IN OUR SOCIETY, thinness is presented as the royal road to success, love and happiness. Martha, who introduced herself with "Hi, I'm a recovered anorexic," had this to say about the promised rewards of thinness:

> I'm so angry when I see things like "Is this how you should look?" I remember a commercial on TV about some kind of drink, crystal mix, I think. They say, "It's only five calories a glass." And they sing some little jingle as they go dancercising across the room, something like "I believe in counting every calorie because I believe in me." I see that and I get furious because I know what they can do to people. They can start thinking, "I'm no good the way I am, so maybe if I become like them people will like me."

Martha grew up in a small town, in a family that was able to provide basic necessities. She had no contact with people from the well-to-do classes until she was in her early teens. Her parents were in their forties when she was born. Her father, now retired, worked for years as a trucker; he also farmed his own land. Both her parents completed grade ten in the local school. Martha's mother wanted to go on to study home economics, but her father said she had to find a job. She worked in a factory during the war and later in the 1960s, when Martha was three years old, took a job as a waitress.

Martha's parents lived in what seemed to be for Martha a beautiful, large, old house they purchased before she was born. Even though she loved the house, she said, "There were times when it felt like a prison," because there was no place to go in the small town. If she was not allowed to go any place or to do something, or felt rejected, Martha would say, "Nobody loves me any more." When her mother was working, Martha's grandfather took care of her, because her grandmother was also working. They played checkers, but there wasn't much else to do.

Martha saw little of her father; he was busy working in his job and on the farms. Yet her father was very affectionate. When she was cold at night, she often cuddled up with him. Martha's mother did all of the housework besides working four days a week, until Martha grew big enough to help her. Martha liked baking and shopping with her mother, whom she described as a "quiet, affectionate, warm and very shy person." Although her mother seemed to care little about fashion, she always wore a little powder and lipstick. She was often tense and, during a period when the family had particularly severe financial problems, she took tranquilizers. Martha recalled that her mother hated "blow ups" and "kept everything to herself.... If there was any tension between ... [the parents], it was never spoken."

Martha was "a skinny little kid" until she hit puberty. She was very picky about what she ate, because there was hardly any food that would not cause her stomach pains. She was scared of eating for fear of the pain. Yet she tried to eat as much as she could lest her mother tell her, "Eat up your dinner; clean up your plate; ... think of the starving children of Biafra."

The family ate lunch and dinner together — it was "always eat and run," for the parents had to rush off to work. Meals were simple, and there was little snack food around. They never had any wine with the meals nor did they keep alcohol in the house.

Martha's family could not afford to take vacations, and they celebrated only Christmas and Thanksgiving.

Throughout her childhood and adolescence, it felt to Martha as if she were an only child. There were no children her age around. (The next sibling is eight years her senior.) She spent a lot of time by herself and often felt bored. When her parents were away — this was most days, most of the time — Martha "really felt unloved." Her first year of school was a pleasant change, because she was finally with other children. That year she attended a one-classroom school house that had only two first-graders. She liked studying and did well. The second year, however, the school was closed down, and the children had to attend a large school ten miles away. This was the first time that Martha was with a lot of children her age. She said she "didn't know how to be with little kids" — she was used to adults. She remembered being "picked on a lot." She was "smart and small," and she was teased for her brain, for her clothes, for being small and skinny. She had no friends. She started staying in the classroom at recesses and at lunch time, and recalled "hanging out with the teacher.... Anything to get away from those rotten little kids." She "hated the politics of being a child," but she "loved to study and loved the learning." She did well in all subjects, but she "was crummy in athletics, in any kind of games and running."

In grades five through seven, Martha was in a special class for gifted children. She participated in the chess club, in plays and singing, but she preferred to work on school projects alone. She still had no real friends and felt like a social outcast. She was hanging out with classmates she describes as "the reject kids: one little girl who was mentally retarded, one who was really fat" and Martha, who was the smallest, skinniest smart kid. She remembered wanting so badly to belong and to be loved, and it just would not happen."

Martha felt particularly miserable in seventh grade. Other girls in her class were beginning to develop breasts and hips. By then

Martha was "tall and skinny," with "not much in either direction." She remembered being taunted with "flatsies":

> I remember on TV they advertised some little balls that were flat, they called them flatsies and that's what they taunted me with, and I remember that really getting to me. I couldn't wait, I thought I'd never grow up.

She missed much of grade seven — pretending to be sick. "The peer pressure got really heavy duty," and she was usually left out. For years, Martha had read every issue of *Miss Chatelaine*, but she did not have clothes that even slightly resembled those in the magazines. She "had a crush on a boy" — this was the focus of her life at the time — but Martha could not seem to get him interested at all. She knew she did not fit in with other children, partly because of the clothes she wore:

> They'd tease me about the clothes I wore. My parents, being older, did not realize that kids were starting to get into fashion, and I had a lot of hand-me-down stuff. I was probably the last one in my class to wear blue jeans.

While she had some idea of stylish dress, Martha didn't seem to be aware of the requirements of ladylike attractiveness until a woman moved next door to their house in the working-class small town and introduced her to a life-style that contained some elements of high fashion elegance. When Martha was about twelve, the house next door was purchased by "a woman from the city." She and her children had many friends who used the house as a ski chalet. This was the first time Martha met "city folks" and well-to-do people. This family "adopted" her. For the first time in her life Martha felt accepted by a group of children; she found a sport (skiing) that she liked and was good at. Although, even with these people, she "never quite got over feeling a little bit like an outsider." Yet meeting this family was particularly important in Martha's life. Through this woman, she became exposed to images of being a woman that were quite different from what she had known. She saw this woman and others who spent time in her house as very attractive, pleasant, in control of their lives, and constantly trying to please men. In a few years, Martha's chief concern in life became attracting and pleasing men through offering her body for sex.

Martha considered this woman and the others from the city to be the embodiment of femininity. They all seemed "exotic, loving and fashionable." They had *Vogue, Cosmopolitan* and a lot of other magazines in their house. As Martha described,

> The woman was really obsessed with appearance and clothes. She didn't have that much money, though. She'd go into Q [an expensive women's clothing store] and buy something, take it home, make a copy of it, and take it back to the store and say she didn't like it. So, I had my first revelation about fashion and the fashion world, and I always had been fashion-conscious, I guess. But this was high fashion. Looking through those magazines I got into the whole trip because of those people. It was the quality, the type of life I'd never seen before. I considered it better than what I could possibly be doing.

The neighbours' and her friends' lives consisted of entertainment and men — or so it seemed. Martha began to dream about a life that included having a "big time" in the city, going out to "trendy places," vacationing, visiting ski resorts and having affairs with popular and attractive men. Although being married did not surface as part of her fantasies at the time, relationships with men were central to the successful and happy life Martha envisioned.

Martha went to a large high school. She described her first two years there as "weird": she "went from being a smart kid to being a rough kid." Her grades fell and she became "really defiant." She "hung out with a group that was into smoking" — she thought it was "cool." She traveled to Europe one summer when she was fifteen with a girl friend, and the two of them spent nearly all their time with a rock band. The following two summers she hung out with a band that was playing in a nearby town.

During these two years Martha was depressed much of the time. She had slept with nearly everyone in the band, including some of the men's friends. She had realized that now she had "something to offer men" and hoped that one of them would care for her, because she had something to give them. She remembered feeling "desperate to be loved, but nothing happened"; no one fell in love with her. As Martha put it, "I wanted them to love me, to think that I was O.K., but the more I gave them the less they thought of me."

It was not until the following year that Martha met someone who reciprocated her desire to be involved. During this relationship, Martha's grades began to improve, she "settled down" and started thinking of attending university. She loved literature and history and wanted to be a writer. Her boyfriend, however, was not willing to "wait around" until she finished her studies. They broke up, and it was then that Martha "quit eating" for the first time. Martha did not stop eating completely, but she cut out many foods and did not eat in front of others so they would all see how upset she was about the break-up. In two weeks her boyfriend returned, having heard that Martha was "cracking up," but the relationship "ended with a big fight."

During the summer that followed Martha began to develop physically and gained about fifteen pounds. As her body started to look more like the body of a woman and she gained some weight, she thought she was "getting fat." Her New Year's resolution at age sixteen was to go on a diet. Martha recalled:

> At that time Maureen Haughton modeled in the *Vogue* a lot. I wanted to look like her. I had this picture of her on my wall. There was one picture of her in a bathing suit. She's got the thinnest inner thighs in the business.... Little did I realize that I could diet till I disappeared and I still would not look like her or anyone else for that matter.

In the next ten months Martha went from a 122 pounds to 78 pounds and was hospitalized. Martha explained as follows:

> What happened was that I'd always been a skinny kid.... If somebody had said to me, it's natural to be gaining some weight; it'll be redistributed; it's the stomach first.... But nobody had told

me that. It's like I wasn't clued in there at all. And so, I just thought I was getting fat and started dieting.

Martha began to read books on dieting. She had a book checked out of the library until she memorized all the calorie counts. She kept track of anything she ate during the day, "added the calories up and kept it under 1,000. Sometimes it'd be 600 or 560." She recalled:

> I figured out what I could eat to make up the calories and just eat that. I ate a lot of lettuce. Once my weight went down to between eighty and ninety; it fluctuated a lot. And then, at the end of the summer I started to push. I wanted to get below 80 lbs. I was 5'4" then.

When I asked Martha what sorts of reactions she got from people when she was losing weight, she said,

> First it was "You look great!" I was wearing size 7 and I was really into fashion. I had a pea green jump suit and everyone loved it. It was gorgeous. I wore really fashionable clothes. It was about the time that the Annie Hall look was really in. I wore a lot of pants with pleats and vests and I wore ties a lot.

The nurse at school started to notice that something was wrong, because she saw Martha going into her office to weigh herself, sometimes twice a day, and Martha was also complaining to her about being constipated. She never took any laxatives, though, remembering her earlier experience with spastic colon, which was very painful. Nor did Martha ever make herself throw up — she simply could not, she said. The school nurse gave Martha an article out of a magazine on anorexia. What she read was all very familiar to Martha: she had been withdrawn, she had not been eating, she was obsessed with her school work, and she was exercising a lot. She worked out in her room regularly and cycled at least six miles a day.

When Martha took home the article the nurse gave her and told her mother, "I think I got anorexia," her mother said, "No, you don't!" Martha thought her mother did not want to believe that her daughter was a "mental case." She felt that her mother responded this way because — as she explained — "Country people consider mental illness worse than physical illness. They don't quite understand it; it's mysterious; and also they figure it's their fault." But Martha's parents could not deny for very long that something was really wrong:

> I remember one night [my father] was looking at me shivering by the wood stove; I was cold all the time. And he said — this is a country expression — "You are as poor as wood, girl," meaning, you're not flesh and blood any more; you're sick; you're in rough shape, kid.

During this period, Martha felt very depressed. She could recall only one time when she laughed, watching something on television that struck her as really funny. Her mother came rushing into the living room and said, "You're laughing! I haven't heard you laugh in such a long time!" Martha described this period as follows:

> [It was] like being down in a hole; you can't see up and around; you're just sitting there in the dark. Time got really weird for me. I had to have every moment planned because unstructured time meant terror. I would see a week-end stretching in front of me like a big black abyss, and I'd think, how am I going to make it till Monday?

Why was this happening to Martha? When I asked her if she thought at the time about how come she was feeling so down, she said, "No. When you're that far down, you're beyond thinking 'how come.' It's just there. You don't see any possible way of ever being anything else."

Martha could not see then that the way she felt had much to do with her having internalized the message: it is only through a man that she would become a person of worth. As Martha said in the interview, without a man, a man's "love," she would be "nothing." When I asked her what she thought would happen to her if she gained more weight, she said:

> Basically that men would not like me, I'd be unattractive.... My whole way of building self-esteem, as much as there was, was sexual. That if a man made love to me, if a man loved me, that would build me up. If I had gotten fat, they would not do that, and how would I feel good about myself then?

This notion, of course, is not unique to Martha. Liz, Katrina and Simone all lived it, although their concrete, day-to-day actions in this regard differed from Martha's. They all worked relentlessly to become fashionably thin. They all wanted to be thin in order to be "eligible," to be noticed, to be treated as women, to have a future that more or less corresponded to the ideals that have been upheld for women.

It is important to note that the ideal of femininity toward which all the interviewed women have lived is an ideal whose realization is a costly undertaking. Yet, this ideal is presented to women as if all women have the same financial resources and could achieve it to the same degree. This is clearly not the case. Martha experienced this contradiction as "not quite fitting in" with the neighbour's children and her friends. She noticed that she did not have the clothing they had nor the traveling experience that they did. Further, she also noted that she learned how to buy relatively inexpensive clothing that "looked good" and made her appear attractive:

> I got really into clothes even though I did not have a lot of money. They call that "fashion sense" now. It actually served me well because now I can do an entire wardrobe with very little money.

Women learn to develop a "fashion sense" as a way to attract the "right-calibre" men. But most women cannot afford to wait for the few princes in the world. Most men work and sweat and live much the same way as their fathers have. One such man will likely marry them, and they will have to clean, cook, wash and change diapers — and maybe also work in a factory or wait tables in a restaurant, like Martha's mother did.

Martha, Liz and Judith are not from middle-class families, but they did not come from the poorest of families either. They all had enough to eat, except for Liz in her early teens, when she was often hungry because her mother did not want her to eat more. The three families had enough income not to dissuade their daughters from aspiring for a university education. With the exception of Liz, they were given some financial support for their studies. Furthermore, Martha — like Simone and Judith — was a last born child, several years younger than her next sibling. By the time Martha, Judith and Simone reached their teens, the other children had left home or they were getting ready to leave. The parents were more comfortable financially by then. It was also a time of economic growth in Canada. These circumstances, together with a set of sociocultural practices beyond the family that touch the core of women's lives, made it possible for these women to be engaged in the relentless pursuit of thinness.

Like Simone, Martha was most pleased with herself when she was able to see the tangible results of her struggle to be thin. They both spoke of the exhilaration they felt when they saw their bones (clavicles, ribs, etc.) sticking out. Martha recalled:

> I remember being able to lie in the bathtub on my stomach, and I could lie there with either hipbone on the bottom of the tub and nothing else touching. My stomach was just flat. And I remember thinking it was reassuringly virtuous that I could be that thin, that I could control myself to the point of being that thin.

As Martha was losing weight and fitting into fashionable (although inexpensive) size 7 clothing, for the first time people started complimenting her on her appearance. The more weight she lost, however, the more she withdrew from people. Her time was totally filled with thinking about her diet, calories, exercising, and her studies. She said that she became "obsessive about school work, and ... wanting to be the best." She became "very self-righteous." She would say to others things like, "How can you eat this stuff? It's not good for you. How can you waste your time doing this or that?" Even her best friend completely withdrew from her because, as Martha recalls, she was "impossible to live with."

As she was losing weight, Martha felt not only virtuous, but also "pure, somehow — when you feel empty, you somehow equate those two things," she said. When I asked her to tell me more about feeling empty, she said:

> When you're not eating very much you're hungry. In that twisted state of mind you feel somehow pure.... It's like I was taking my emotions and stashing them somewhere. I was having a hard time dealing with my emotions.

Early in her life Martha learned not to be "lazy or mouthy." She had to behave in a way that would not be disapproved of by neighbours. When she was very young, Martha learned many things from one brother, including the importance of being honest. This brother was highly respected and admired by the parents. Martha wanted to become like her brother: "really thin and tall, smart, unemotional." Martha thought that maybe she had been the reject in the family because she was so unlike her brother, who was aloof, calm, collected. Martha was quite different:

> I was so emotional, so outgoing, so sensitive to things going on around me, and I thought that's what's getting me into so much trouble. That when I love somebody I show it, and when I am angry I show it, and that's just not a good thing to be doing. I wanted to be more like him, and I did become like him. I was very withdrawn.

Expression of strong emotions was discouraged in all of the interviewed women's families. Expressing feelings passionately, but especially angrily, was taken to be a sign of revolt — and was prohibited.

Families like Martha's are not abnormal. It is the exception rather than the rule in white North American and Western European society that parents encourage their daughters to speak their minds and to show how they feel. Girls have to conform and submit themselves to authority figures (represented at first by the parents) much more than boys do. The parents are not mean and cruel; they try to teach their daughters what they have seen and believe to be important preparation for their lives. Polite coldness (more recently, cruel coldness), aloofness and emotional detachment in general are encouraged in the world outside the walls of the home, and those who do not learn to conform to this rule are usually severely penalized — particularly if they are women. The polite, submissive expressions — defined as "pleasant" or "proper" manners for girls — sometimes transform into numbness, a feeling that was at times much desired by Simone and other suffering women. They also place women in the position of pleasing men, of self-valuation through the other. Martha talked about reading Erica Jong's *Fear of Flying* at age fourteen — she read a lot of novels, "sexy novels." But she thinks it was *Fear of Flying* that was the turning point in her life — turning toward men:

> The magazines, like *Cosmopolitan*, with articles on how to please your man, how to find a man, how to date men, how to turn men on — my parents were never into that; my mother wasn't; she never dressed up in any particular way.... Also, this woman next door .... She was single and had been married a couple of times. She was very concerned with what men thought of her, and pleasing men and attracting men. If there were men in the house she'd be waiting on them hand and foot.

These sociocultural practices are intertwined with the popular media's treatment of women. The media do not merely reflect reality; they create reality as well:

> The lights are dimmed in the college auditorium and we watch the slides, frightening both in their numbers and source (popular women's magazines). We see a woman bound and blindfolded in

Vogue. We see a Christian Dior ad of a woman under the foot of a man. We see an Esprit ad of a woman prone on an ironing board, a man running an iron across her stomach. (Faludi 1988, 52)

Woman bound and blindfolded .... Woman under man's foot .... Woman's stomach flat as an ironing board — as Martha's stomach once was. Our practices and our knowledge are shaped by such images. What we know — especially in North America — we know from the popular media that has created certain images and desires and impel us toward certain actions. The images of femininity cannot be separated from the contents of popular women's magazines — the magazines Martha saw in her city-woman neighbour's house. Liz and Martha read the same magazines and watched many of the same programs on television as Simone did, and as even Katrina did in South America.

Still, women's pursuit of thinness — one component of attractive appearance — cannot be understood in isolation from sexuality, work and class. Women's class location demarcates the possibilities of the specific work they perform inside and outside the home and, thus, defines the particular modes of their sexual exploitation. Yet women's appearance provides a point of entry into this complex interrelationship since part of the work of women (regardless of occupation) is making themselves attractive — attractive to men for marriage, work and subsistence. An entire social structure creates the possibilities of, endorses, derives profits from and depends on women's feminization, and, because women actually die in the relentless pursuit of thinness, their deaths.

Although media instruct women consistently in what to consider proper, desirable and possible for them, we need to understand more fully how it is that women (and men) *desire* certain life-styles and value certain goals and achievements but not others. How can we explain what has happened to Martha, Simone, Liz and other women without either blaming them for having been weak or maladaptive or treating them as simply victims of female socialization? Such analyses must draw upon concrete examples of processes in which women's subjectivity is neither disembodied nor decontextualized. We need to ask: How are everyday and popular media discourses intertwined in the pursuit of attractive appearance? How do romances of various forms (movies, novels) co-constitute this pursuit? How do we understand the assumptions of heterosexuality and marriage in this construction? How are these assumptions sustained in the pursuit of attractive appearance? We need to explicate further the ideological practices and processes concerted by all social institutions and the contradictions they produce to arrive at a more complete and concrete appraisal of women's situations.

Martha began dieting to attract and please men and went on for nearly a year. She had to keep losing weight for, even though she had lost a lot by the time she weighed 90 pounds, she still did not have the body, love and lifestyle she was looking for.

Martha, like all women who have internalized the messages, learned that she should aspire for the life-style of the rich and famous. It would be important to have a fashionable apartment, to eat leisurely meals of expensive foods and wines, and to go out to "trendy places." She learned that women should dress according to the latest styles in "high fashion" and should strive to take expensive vacations and frequent ski resorts, seeking the company of attractive and popular men. In order to keep such company, we must be exotic and loving, as well as pleasing to men.

Martha's ideas about her future as a woman were shaped, to a large degree, by the sophisticated city woman living next door — a woman who lived by the magazine images of women. Martha, similar to Liz, Katrina and Simone, spent much of her life working towards becoming attractive and thin and treating her body primarily as an object for others. The objectification of the body becomes alienation from the body when turned against oneself, yet that was the only course of action Martha could follow in her desperate attempt to be somebody. Although seeking men's love was a theme present in the interviews with all the previous women, in Martha's case this search for men's love was most explicitly tied to offering her body for men's sexual pleasure. For a period in Martha's life, making her body available to men was her sole means of achieving any sense of self-worth. When she found herself gaining weight, it seemed to her that she was losing her only possibility to be cared for by a man.

Martha recalled that she talked very little with her mother when she was young, but one of the earliest conversations she could remember was about marriage. She was told that as a white girl she could not marry a Black man because their children would not belong to either group. As a child, Martha was also taught that around age twenty a girl should be married, but, as she put it, she "could not see beyond the pretty dress."

Martha, similar to the other interviewed women, was caught between a number of conflicting values, ideals and aspirations. She heard, on the one hand, that she should strive for leading a simple life-style. On the other hand, she was surrounded by images of the life of the wealthy. These images shaped her desires and aspirations. That Martha sought a sense of self-worth exclusively through sexual relations with men for a period in her life is also bound up with the images in which she was immersed in a media-dominated society. The promise of the messages of main-stream culture was that if she had the appearance of those women who were presented as loved, happy and successful, she would also have it all.

Martha, along with Liz, Katrina and Simone, was aware of having to fit in, to be like other popular women. This, too, was a conflict-ridden goal for, simultaneous with fitting in, the women all knew that they also had to stand out if they were to be noticed by men. Both fitting in and standing out are defined, primarily, in terms of appearance — the appearance of the woman's body, her actions and speech. In this society, appearance is the most important dimension of many people's heterosexual relationships. The relationship itself may be best described as an appearance.

As she was growing up, Martha was taught much the same set of social values as Simone, Judith and the other women interviewed. One set of values she learned was having to be a good daughter. Good daughters help their mothers with housework. They obey their parents. Mothers and daughters should share good times together, (e.g., shop and bake together). Perfect daughters are treated with affection by their parents and siblings. They act in ways that do not bring about the disapproval or criticisms of neighbours and friends. A good girl eats up her food, even if she is full. She takes responsibility for choosing a vocation or career for herself.

A good daughter observes her parents values, which include living a simple life. She collects no debts, and she buys only what she can pay for by cash. She strives to acquire the basic necessities in life, such as a nice home and simple, functional clothing. She is honest and works hard to achieve what she wants. She marries within her own racial group to avoid upsetting traditional views. She keeps her feelings to herself, particularly feelings of pain, shame, disapproval, criticism and anger. She is in control of all facets of her life.

As Martha learned, a good daughter is also virtuous, that is, better than others. She exercises self-control (by dieting) to the utmost. She fills up her time with useful activities. She works very hard to repent her weaknesses. She tries to educate others about their mistaken ways and bad habits. She experiences purity by practicing self-restraint. However, to fit in, she should also seek fun. It is fun (cool) to smoke dope and hang out with entertainers. Going on ski trips, having nights out in restaurants and bars and watching the soaps on television are fun.

A woman must show her vulnerability at the break up of a relationship. If she does not express graphically the severity of her pain — by starving herself, for instance — it means she is not really suffering. It is not acceptable to feel depressed; a woman should find ways of keeping her spirit up, including having sex with men even if she does not feel like it. It is also her responsibility to prevent pregnancy.

Through her own painful experiences, Martha has become aware of many contradictions in these values, contradictions lived by women including herself, and of some of the roots of these contradictions. It took Martha a year to recover her weight. During this time she dreamed of high class, high fashion, going out to trendy places in town, a life-style that included weekends at ski resorts, romances with ski instructors, sipping good wine, etc. It took longer than a year for her to cease to be so totally concerned with the importance of her appearance and to discover that she may not be "the smartest, the most beautiful and the strongest," but she could still be "quite acceptable" to herself. Therapy and readings about women's issues helped Martha to make this discovery.

She was fortunate to find a therapist — and a very good one — shortly after she began losing weight. Many other women in similar situations have been far less lucky. It is estimated that at present, in Toronto, one in twelve adolescent girls suffers from an eating disorder (Dineen 1987, B1-B2). There is a severe shortage of treatment opportunities for girls and women in the relentless pursuit of thinness, and no training centres exist for therapists interested in working with such women. The rare openings for therapy that can be found are prohibitive in cost for most women in desperate need. This situation must be rectified immediately.

But we must also ask: What kind of treatment will be offered for women in need? What kind of training will these therapists have? How will therapists interpret the relentless pursuit of thinness? And what will be the goals of treatment? A not unusual report of a therapeutic "success story" reads as follows:

> When she curls her hair and puts on her tight designer jeans, she looks like any other fashionably underweight 17-year-old girl (though rather more beautiful), except perhaps for the eyes which

are older, wiser and sadder than any teenager's have a right to be.

Twice each week, Jane drives her new T-roof Mustang into Manhattan for a therapy session .... Jane's anorexic personality has not altogether faded. (Fadiman 1982, 76)

According to this report in *Life Magazine*, when a woman who has been suffering from anorexia nervosa gains weight and exhibits the appearance and practices typically associated with a woman making herself attractive to men, she is considered to be recovering or almost recovered. It seems that one goal of Jane's therapy was to enhance and maintain her feminine appearance and foster her desirability to men. Jane also happens to be a woman who has access to a life-style that few can afford. Few can pay for the individual sessions with a renowned specialist and drive to his office in a new Mustang. As this example shows, the golden-girl image of anorexia nervosa continues to be propagated by the media, despite researchers' warnings about its dangers (Garner 1983a & 1983c). This image suggests that success, wealth, love and happiness go hand in hand with the relentless pursuit of thinness. To cite another example from *Starweek Magazine*,

At 22, Tracey Bregman is the kind of young woman most teenage girls dream of becoming — beautiful, talented, successful, well known.... But three years ago, in an effort to become an even more perfect version of herself, Tracey began abusing her body via those twin eating disorders, anorexia nervosa ... and bulimia .... (Sellers 1985, 4)

Like the woman Chernin (1981) described in the locker room who wanted to "contract" anorexia nervosa to become thin, many women have been taught to think that through this condition their possibilities for success, fame and love will somehow be enhanced. Such ideas are presented daily in all the media. They also present eating disorders as pathologies of individual minds, which they are not, and I doubt that these messages can be successfully eradicated merely by individual or family therapies. Yet, the reported stories of anorexic women (who are nearly always famous figures) appear to suggest that an underlying personality disturbance is responsible for the condition. Tracey, in the above example, was said to suffer from perfectionism, others from an overwhelming sense of inadequacy, inferiority or lack of control in their lives. The same is said about bulimic women: "Bulimics tend to be high achievers who demand perfection in everything they do" (*McGill News* Fall 1987, 10). And, speaking of women with eating disorders, Joan E. Enoch, Medical Director of the first residential treatment centre for anorexia nervosa and bulimia in the United States, notes, "Because *they* are never satisfied with the way they look and the shape of their bodies, they make a marathon effort to feel more presentable" (Enoch 1987, 1). It is unsettling to hear an expert in a leading treatment facility address women's dissatisfaction with their bodies as an internal-personal problem that affected other women — as if the therapists themselves did not experience much the same dissatisfaction with their own bodies.

Most therapies, sometimes perhaps inadvertently, reinforce the notion that the crux of the illness is one or another form of imperfection to be overcome by *individual* effort. Paradoxically, the client then has to become perfect at being imperfect.

The counsellor or therapist, like everyone else in society, approaches her or his work from a certain perspective that is laden with a particular view of the world, including specific value judgements (Strupp 1974). As Jane's example suggests, the therapist also makes certain judgements about the meaning of a client's actions and their implications for social relations. But the therapist cannot — and should not — have a concrete plan for the restructuring of the client's life or for how it will be lived concretely (Bors & Szekely 1981). To offer such a plan would amount to substituting one form of objectification and exploitation with another.

In our media-dominated society, the therapist, like the client, is immersed in prescriptions for what is normal, healthy and desirable. When a therapist advocates that an anorexic client curl her hair and put on tight designer jeans, she or he testifies to having subscribed to dominant sociocultural images of femininity. No space is provided for the client to find and create her own images or to act according to those that would be liberating for her.

It is exceedingly difficult for the therapist to be aware of the social constitution of the relentless pursuit of thinness, or of the importance of appearance in general. Yet, in the absence of critical reflection on such issues, the therapist is likely to help perpetuate women's oppression by making the socially accepted appearance and behaviours of women the goal of treatment — as we have seen in the above example about Jane. The therapist's task is continually to seek to understand how our ideals, values and aspirations are socially constituted and to integrate this awareness into her work with clients in the relentless pursuit of thinness.

The same point applies concerning the issue of how to prevent women's struggles to be fashionably thin. The issue of prevention must be raised at the level of education, where education is understood in radically social terms. Today's girls and boys need to begin to study social history; they need to learn to ask questions about their situations, and they need truthful answers, not myths. They must come to the realization that health is not an individual issue, it is a social-political issue.

Women need to learn their particular histories, as Martha has begun to do. They must be given the tools to understand the ground of the possibility of such practices as the relentless pursuit of thinness. They must come to recognize their situations — actual or potential — in the plight of the starving anorexic women. They must challenge the social structures that limit the spaces women have been allowed to occupy. Women must come to see that the present political-economic structure has everything to gain from treating their appearances as commodities and depriving them of their rights.

With or without the help of therapists, some women have begun to challenge the images of attractiveness and the prescriptions of femininity. Last year a group of women came together in Toronto to form a group called "Hersize." They are a "weight prejudice action group" for people for whom food is no longer a form of social control, who can eat chocolate chip cookies without feeling guilty or regretful about every bit they swallow. They "want to increase public awareness of fat oppression and free women from being overly concerned with body size and shape" (Sweet 1988, D1) Their first action as a group was to challenge an ad for a new book that promoted bulimia as a means of weight loss. They monitor magazines, newspapers and television programs for their portrayal of women; they challenge multimillion-dollar businesses depicting women as if we were all one size — small and slim.

Other women have come forward publicly, describing themselves as "obese, rotund, fat" — and liking themselves (Zarzour 1987a, L1). There are now workshops offered to women to help them accept their body size and not to judge their own worth based on how much they weigh or what their physical shape is. Many of these women have been highly successful in their jobs, yet they have felt their lives have been ruined because of their size or shape. Some of them have tried as many as eight different diets a year — every year since adolescence, and none ever worked. For these women it takes tremendous struggle to learn to let go of the ideal of the fashion model's body, to be able to feel fine as fat women. Like Simone and Judith, these women have often, since their childhood, been insulted by family and total strangers for their size. For the first time, some of them are now walking with a sense of dignity and pride they did not know before.

To cite one other example, Ann Simonton has been fighting for years against the commercial exploitation of women. As a former fashion model, Simonton knows from personal experience that "... women are displayed like pieces of meat for corporate profit" (Faludi 1988, 34). She graphically made this point when she walked down the streets of Santa Cruz wearing an outfit made of thirty pounds of bologna and pimiento loaf. The necklace and crown she wore were made of hot dogs. In striking contrast to the glamourized images of fashion models, Simonton said that, at the peak of her career, "I was nothing more than a mannequin.... I was a nobody" (ibid., 52). She quit modeling and produced a slide show, "Sex, Power and the Media," which she presents across the United States on her speaking tours. She has taken part in protests and demonstrations against beauty pageants, pornography and other forms of exploitation of women's bodies. At the "Myth California" protest a few years ago, she chained a bathroom scale to her ankle and jumped through Hula Hoops labeled "Beauty Obedience School" as a way to demonstrate "Weight Slavery" (ibid., 34). She wants women to "take personal responsibility for being the accomplice" — like she was while modeling — in their own objectification (ibid., 54).

Myths about dieting and "healthy weight" have finally begun to be challenged. We can now hear that slimness is not a sign of health, that women between 5'3" and 5'6" weighing between 115 and 194 pounds are equally healthy on average (Zarzour 1987b, L6). We are beginning to be told that being underweight is as much a health risk as being overweight, that in terms of health what matters most is having a stable weight. We can now sometimes read that dieting perpetuates dieting; that after a diet nearly all people gain weight, even while consuming the same number of calories; that they become preoccupied with food. To counter the diet craze, we need to hear much more of this type of information. We need to be presented with accepted and acceptable images of women of all physical shapes and sizes and races. We need to see women's worth being based on what they *do*, not on what they look like.

Martha is one of the minority of women who are recovered anorexics — almost. For, as she noted,

> The vestiges of anorexia [are] ... still there ... — the concern with appearance, the concern with my weight, [even] as much as I say I

happen to be very fond of my pot belly and I don't really care how I look. People can love me the way I am or they can go…. I know that's sort of the correct thing to say and that's what I said [before]. But I'm beginning to realize that it's like recovering from alcoholism. You're always dealing with the issues that caused it. I know that I'd never ever go back to being anorexic because I just couldn't do that again. There's no way. *I'm too militant and angry about what it does to people.*

But then she went on to say,

There are times when I'm depressed or have been rejected by someone in a relationship — and I think, I'll just lose weight. And then I think, "Don't be stupid; you did that once, and look where it's got you." It still comes to my mind. I'm still concerned with my figure. I am concerned that I am — I think I am average, but according to charts and fashion — I am way over average.

I asked Martha about the times when she thinks, "I'll just lose weight." Does that mean that she does not feel attractive to men? She said,

Yes. Also, sometimes it's I'll show them. I'll just get skinny again…. I internalize their rejection as being my fault and I figure I'll strike back by hurting myself — to make them feel bad…. I can say I still got the problem because I deal with it every day.

Martha has come to recognize the ways in which media images of women have shaped her experiences. She spoke angrily about what happened to her and felt frustrated at seeing others going through the same experiences:

I think about young women, the twelve-fourteen-years old, who watch TV and read magazines, and are affected by that kind of thing. I'm worried more about them. I've gone through it and have dealt with it, but they are the ones who are going down now.

The media messages Martha was referring to are much like the ones to which she was exposed prior to and at the height of her starvation months. She said it was the anger at the realization that she had been "sucked into a vast scheme" that helped her stay alive and, eventually, got her interested in feminism. Martha connected the commercial mythology of the perfect woman directly to everyday life — hers and other women's:

> I don't know how many times I have heard this: "Oh, I really should not eat this." Women who don't really need to lose weight are thinking, "I need to lose weight. I am not loved like I am, and somehow if I lose weight I'll be loved ...." It's like a cult, a cult worshipping the physical form of the thin model that seems to be successful and happy and loved.

Women in the relentless pursuit of thinness are victims of a "very destructive force, a subculture that is very strong and dominating. And they can't think critically" about what they are told, Martha said, because " their own self-esteem is so low that they can't seem to see out from under.... When you're worshipping [the thin model], how are you supposed to look at it critically?" It became apparent to her that the thin model came to be worshipped and emulated by women only through their own hope of achieving success, love and happiness.

When Martha questioned the possibility for women to look critically at the idol of the thin model they are worshipping, I shared one of my fantasies of a possible cure with her: literally, take North American or Western European women, who desperately struggle to be thin, to a place that is radically different; then bring them back home so that they can consider anew what the pursuit of thinness is all about. Maybe then, I thought, women would see and refuse the scheme. To my surprise, Martha said,

> I did, actually, go away. I went to [X] for two years, and there I learned to accept myself a lot more. I was in a quite remote area. I lived very close to the land. There wasn't a fashion push.... I was removed from main-stream city social life. It really built me up to believe in myself, too, because I lived under very difficult circumstances. It was physically difficult ... no water, no electricity. It was really good for me. I wasn't the strongest person in the world, or the smartest, but I wasn't the weakest or the stupidest either.

But I think, as far as opening my eyes went, it was ... [the therapy] and feminism. Actually, it turned out to be one of the most positive experiences in my life because I know I'll never get that far down again because of the understanding I now have. And it also made me see that almost everybody has emotional problems; everybody has a cross to bear.

As Martha re-evaluated her life and aspirations, attracting men ceased to be her sole channel of activity. She accepted that she might not be the most sexually desired woman or number one in any pursuit, but she could work and be involved in activities from which she derived a sense of worth and satisfaction. She no longer needed to depend on men to acknowledge and value her merely because of her sexual function. She now refers to "*Cosmo*" and other women's magazines as "trash" and laughs at the images of a "trendy" life-style that just a few years ago were so close to her heart. She has begun to think of men not as ultimate validators of her worth, but as potential friends and partners. Now, Martha's sense of her own worth is grounded much more in her ability to work, study and ask questions about the world than in her skills at making herself desirable to men.

More than any of the other women interviewed, Martha has been able to see the pursuit of thinness from critical perspectives previously unfamiliar to her. At the time when she started to diet, Martha weighed 122 pounds. Her weight fell below 100 pounds and she still felt that she had to go on dieting. She struggled with exercising and depriving herself of food — until she weighed in at the seventy pounds range. Today, heavier than at the beginning of her first diet, Martha is angry:

This society is killing its people; it's killing its women. "If you can't conform to this image we don't want you!" To someone who is like me! And that's just average, right? *And that's somehow not good enough!?*

CHAPTER SIX

THE BODY
IN SOCIETY

... these girls, far from being glamorous, are seriously ill; and their illness comes into existence because they, like many of the rest of us, have taken up an identity with the mind in opposition to the body. As a result they are pitted against the body and must live out their lives with a determination to inflict their will upon it. Anorexia is, above all, an illness of self-division and can only be understood through this tragic splitting of body from mind. (Chernin 1981, 47).

In all of the clinical literature, including most of the feminist literature as well, the relentless pursuit of thinness is conceptualized as an illness. Even Chernin — who recognized that "many of the rest of us" experience the same kind of split as the girls she described — separated women into anorexic and non-anorexic. In essence, like other other feminists who have wondered whether anorexia could be considered a "true internal psychopathology" (Brown 1985, 61), Chernin also depicted the phenomenon as an illness. I have attempted to move away from such conceptualization, rejecting the view that the medical model is a viable approach to the relentless pursuit of thinness among women. The language of the medical model, however, is so ingrained in our vocabulary that I could not completely avoid using terms such as "anorexia," "eating disorders" and "the relentless pursuit of thinness."

A feminist perspective on this phenomenon is incompatible with the medical model. The medical model should be rejected. Any phenomenon approached from a medical-model framework is quickly decontextualized. Whatever is observed becomes stripped of the actual situation in which the observation is made. The pursuit of thinness, like any other phenomenon, is speedily reduced to the individual — to her weakness, a personality defect or her arrested development. The conceptual scheme of individualistic psychological theories, including a particularly devaluing language, is employed to accomplish this reduction. In the anorexia literature, phrases such as "thought disordered," "literal-minded," "cognitively retarded," "peculiarly oversensitive," "unable to think independently" and suffering from "visual distortions" are frequently used to depict the "affected" woman. Such phrases are scattered throughout Noella Caskey's article, "Interpreting Anorexia Nervosa," for instance. The conceptual framework of these terms is not explained nor is any attention paid to the implications of their usage. The devaluing and pathologizing language used by many authors conceals the genesis and development of the relentless pursuit of thinness. In Caskey's (1986) interpretation, for example, we read that "will alone produces ... and maintains [anorexia nervosa]" (p. 184). Such statements obscure the social-political roots and contribute to the daily perpetuation of women's oppression and exploitation. Furthermore, it has the contradictory effect of normalizing these practices by placing particular women in the category "sick."

The conceptual and language scheme employed serves the purpose of "blaming the victim" (Ryan 1971). The "victim" could be the anorexic daughter, her mother, father or all three of them, but it is always the individual viewed separate from her or his life situation. Since we are social beings, no individual can be understood independently of her situation, including other people. Before someone can say "I" she has to be addressed as "you"; the "I" continuously develops in dialogue with the world. Martha, for example, did not first become who she was and then begin to hang posters of a fashion model on the walls of her room. The two cannot be separated. Rather, she was who she was at that point in her life in conjunction with what these posters of fashion models meant to her in her life situation. Simone was not, initially, an insecure child who was, therefore, particularly bothered by being called "fatty." She came to feel and think about herself in disparaging terms because of the disparaging treatment that fat people, including herself, received. We must avoid interpreting someone's life independently of how a person is treated by numerous others in her life and what her relationships are with actual people as well as with those more impersonal others depicted in the popular media. If we sever the ongoing dialogue and dialectic of these relations, our statements concerning the individual become empty. They only *appear* to reveal something new and meaningful about her. In fact, they merely substitute different words for something we do not understand.

By placing women in the "sick" category, the question — what does this phenomenon reveal about the particular social situation of women in the relentless pursuit of thinness? — can hardly be answered. It is because this question cannot be raised in a meaningful way that Chernin, for example, ends up suggesting that, in relation to the pursuit of thinness, we can distinguish two groups of women: those who fight for "feminine power" and those who "retreat from it" (Chernin 1981, 99). In the face of reality, this either/or of being feminist or anorexic (or potentially anorexic), cannot be maintained. Those who fight for women's rights are also concerned with body image, with being thin and in shape, as portrayed in the media. They also care and worry about their appearance, including their weight. It would be impossible to substantiate the claim that theirs is a healthy concern whereas, by definition, anorexic women's identical concerns are sick. Yet, that is the only argument that could be made. Furthermore, the women who have been called anorexic are also often committed to fighting for women's rights, like other feminists. The ill/not ill dichotomy does not hold up.

In addition to being acontextual, the medical model, and any approach that slides back and forth between claiming to be feminist and borrowing the framework of the medical model, is also ahistorical. Because the phenomenon under investigation has been stripped of the social situation in which it is embedded, its development cannot be traced over time. I use the word "development" here in two interrelated ways: how a practice emerges within the life-span of a specific person, and how the emergence of this practice relates to social-historical processes. Most writers agree that "something happened" in the last two decades that is related to the increasing concern women have expressed about their bodies' weight and size. Attempts to explicitly bring into play the sociocultural factor is an indication of this recognition. Once a phenomenon has, however, been constructed as a disease, the sociocultural can only be viewed as a factor that further undermines the weak personality of the individual. Such a conclusion is inevitable if the starting point for the understanding of the individual is not a social one. Ultimately, researchers end up looking within the isolated individual for an underlying explanation of her weakness.

The question of why this particular woman becomes so preoccupied with the relentless pursuit of thinness is the kind that has been asked about all the other conditions that have been deemed psychiatric. Schizophrenia is a prime example of searching for individual and family variables to explain an illness and, ultimately, attempting to establish the genetic cause: "What is it about the biology of the individual schizophrenic that predisposes him or her toward the disorder" (Rose, Kamin & Lewontin 1984, 3202). The search for a genetic explanation, along with offering psychotropic drugs as cure for anorexia nervosa, has already begun (Dineen 1987). Rose, Kamin and Lewontin (1984) assert that "an adequate theory of schizophrenia must understand what it is about the social and cultural environment that pushes some categories of people toward manifesting schizophrenic symptoms; it must understand that such social and cultural environments themselves profoundly affect the biology of the individuals concerned ..." (p. 231).

Asking the question, why this rather than that woman falls victim to the relentless pursuit of thinness, typically arises from a reductionistic perspective (be it biological or psychological). It also reflects the dominant ideology of our society: individualism. This question is lodged in self/society dualism as well as in problems of research, theory and practice. The question — why this woman? — is a search for ultimate causes and for removing responsibility from anyone but the affected person. In the interests of those who rule, it simultaneously maintains belief in the generally good, right and just nature of society. This question precludes the investigation of meaningful structural relationships that are likely to shed light on the particular sociocultural conditions in which the possibility of such diverse phenomena as schizophrenia and the relentless pursuit of thinness emerge. It also discourages raising such questions as: what can we grasp about the social organization and distribution of political and economic power when we examine the manner in which psychiatric disorders are viewed and treated? It does away with the need to investigate critically the dialectic of the personal and social, since science promises to offer the final word — the word about our genes. Science, of course, does not make promises about what it can do in isolation from the power relations in which researchers and other experts are trained and research-based industries are financed.

Why this woman rather than another can only be answered if all of the complex interrelationships of the personal, family and sociocultural are investigated without appeal to a final or ultimate cause. Although the study of various aspects of the relentless pursuit of thinness may continue for a long time (depending on resources for researchers), unless we approach the investigation from a perspective that does not attempt to reduce phenomena to one common determinant, these studies will remain isolated fragments, lacking unity and coherence as psychology on the whole does (Koch 1959).

The questions that may be more fruitful to pursue than why this woman include: Why is it thinness women strive for? Which groups of women are more likely to pursue thinness; who and where are they, and how can we identify them? What is revealed about the world in which we live by women's relentless pursuit of thinness and related phenomena? How is this pursuit lived and produced? In what ways is this pursuit an integral aspect of social relations? What is revealed about social relations by the treatment of women in psychiatric and everyday settings, including the media? And, finally, how can we change social relations so that the pursuit of thinness becomes less likely to emerge?

The analysis of the relentless pursuit of thinness among women has made visible a number of contradictions. At the very centre of these contradictions is the human body, our bodies in society. Throughout the analysis, I have sought to present women's bodies in relation to other people and in concrete situations. The major theoretical problem this analysis has revealed to me is our lack of understanding of the body. Neither the clinical (psychiatric/psychological) nor the feminist literature has grappled with this issue adequately.

Nearly all psychiatric/psychological approaches fail to consider that learning is a bodily function, that "... becoming a member of a particular culture is in part becoming a certain sort of body" (Fay 1987, 148). And, "... having a body is, for a living creature, to be involved in a definite social environment, to identify oneself with certain projects and be continually committed to them" (Merleau-Ponty 1962, 82). It is in the process of ongoing learning and commitment to definite projects that our bodies are molded into a certain sort. But once we have taken apart body, cognition, affect and environment — as is typically done in Western social science — how do we put them back together?

As we have seen, feminist writers describe the anorexic and bulimic practices within the broader context of a consumer-oriented economic structure in which patriarchal social relations prevail. They have pointed as well to women's changing roles within this structure as a major area of conflict in Western women's lives. A few authors have attempted to delineate the psychological dynamics of the relationship between parents and daughters with some reference to the larger sociocultural milieu. While these interpretations impel us to pay attention to women's actual life situations which co-constitute bodily practices much more than pervasive clinical/psychiatric views would have us do, they are not without their problems. The body is still not brought fully into the focus of inquiry. The descriptions and analyses of bodies that are provided lack reflexivity — they fail to account for the bodily practices of the theorists, and they also perpetuate fear of speaking/dealing with the body, a tradition that Spelman called "somatophobia in feminist theory" (Spelman 1982, 124).

In addition to evading descriptions of actual bodies, unexamined and conflicting assumptions about the body and human development in general permeate both the clinical/psychiatric and feminist writings. Neither of them have understood development as a sociocultural process in all aspects of an individual's life from its genesis. Neither have taken up in any detail the theoretical and methodological issues that are central to understanding the gendered body. They have not addressed the problems inherent in subject-object dualism and in models that explain behaviour in terms of reacting to socialization processes. Women continue to be depicted as merely responding passively to socio-psychological influences.

In nearly all of the psychological theorizing about the relentless pursuit of thinness, we find that parts of existing theories have been borrowed and then combined with a feminist perspective. For this reason, most writings are plagued with the problems inherent in the borrowed theories. All of these theories are reductionist, dualistic and deterministic. Many theories are also essentialistic in that they postulate a hidden feminine nature, a natural Self, or a system of needs that should determine the course of our lives. Due to early traumatic experiences of disapproval and rejection, however, the expression or actualization of our essential nature, self or need has been said to be blocked. Femininity, self and need are often treated as biological givens. They are not analyzed as subject to the mediation of social-historical processes and practices. Body/self and the social world are treated as two separate domains rather than being integrated from the start. Thus, complex processes of development are reduced to the level of the "vital order," of existence, which could never account adequately for the "human order" (Merleau-Ponty 1963, 129).

In the self-psychological, object-relations and Jungian explanations offered for anorexia, the social character of our existence means little more than the psychodynamics of family relations. Instead of describing these family relations in their lived reality and mapping out the connections among social relations and the concrete events that have occurred in an anorexic woman's life, family dynamics are subjected to speculation at an abstract level. Yet, in the absence of concrete descriptions and analyses (or perhaps because of their absence), all of these theories offer prescriptions for healthy development. In the lack of structural-social-historical analyses, the prescriptions are inevitably static and fixed and cannot offer practical suggestions for how to change the situations that have co-constituted the relentless pursuit of thinness.

One further problem with all of the borrowed theories is their inability to explain the psychological ground for women's resistance (see Sayers 1986). How are we to account for the fact that many women, including several of the authors whose work has been reviewed, have not fallen victim to the global conditions that — in their interpretation — blocked healthy development and led to anorexia? How is it that, despite women's devaluation and the pervasive hostility to women's bodies, not all the women, and not all of the time, behave and experience themselves in ways that would be described as typically feminine? Why would women act in these ways at all? The essentialist reductionism of these theories renders them incapable of answering such questions.

In all of the psychological theories, the tension between active-passive, self-other, subject-object continue to be present in an unresolved and unproblematic manner. There is a theoretical (and methodological) crisis in Western social science and also in feminist psychology. Many feminists have critiqued main(male)-stream science, but few have acknowledged openly that a crisis exists within feminist research itself. Simply saying that the work is written from a feminist perspective cannot serve as a corrective to the shortcomings of the borrowed theories. Feminists have explored the meaning of the female body in, for example, literature about pornography and sexual abuse, as well as in feminist films, but a coherent framework for how to think about the body has not yet emerged. It is precisely the question, how to understand the body as social, in general, and women's body as social, in particular, that is at the core of the problems with the anorexia literature.

How would we begin to find a framework for addressing the body? What would be some of the basic requirements such a framework would have to satisfy? How would we proceed once a framework has emerged?

As obvious as it may sound, we must begin by including the body in whatever it is that we speak about. We must stop talking about mental or cognitive processes as if they were separate from actual people's concrete lives. We have to start by describing people's lives — always in relationships with other persons and objects and always in action.

There are no purely psychological phenomena. Everything we do, feel and think is in a dialectical relation with the world. The conflicts we experience point to conflicts and contradictions in the world; they can never be reduced to figments of the imagination of sick minds, as we often find in the anorexia literature. The sick minds cannot further be reduced to bio-chemical processes. There is no innate or biological realm in itself when we speak of human beings. Differences that exist among people are never simply a given, never simply a trait of a person's racial, sexual or class status. These differences are products of intentional human activity, and, as such, they are always tied to motivating interests.

As feminist psychologists and social scientists, we must locate ourselves in the description of actual people in concrete situations. We must be clear about where we stand in actual relation to what is being described. Our stance may, and in all likelihood will, change as we understand more about what we are trying to depict. At the beginning of this research, I saw myself as totally outside of the lives of the people I wanted to study. I saw myself as unlike them, and it was exactly that awareness that inspired the study. Some common ground has, however, emerged as I began to recognize that anorexia was not something that happened to other women. I have seen certain practices that I share with the women I interviewed. I have caught a glimpse of the social relations that have shaped my own life and helped me live it in a manner that thus far has not necessitated the practices, nor given rise to the kind of relationship to my body, that Simone has, for example. Under different circumstances, however, I could have experienced my body in much the same way that she has. If I were raised in a society where appearance is considered to be women's major asset, where what women are able to do matters far less than what they look like, where people are raised to be never satisfied in the midst of plenty, I too may have struggled to make my body conform to the feminine ideal.

There are a number of serious difficulties in perceiving the body as thoroughly social — in a particular situation and with others. One difficulty is that we forget the body. We have taken the body for granted and are not used to including our own bodies and that of others in social science research. Probyn has pointed out that "... in certain theoretical practices gender-as-problematic has become 'normal,' while the everyday body has disappeared" (Probyn 1987, 118). We have very few words to speak about the body, especially to speak in a manner that does not already fragment the body or categorize it along separate domains of scientific inquiry. As soon as we begin to speak of the body in any detail, we lose the sense of the body as lived (O'Neill 1985). Turner (1984) pointed to the absence of actual bodies in sociological inquiries. In most social science theorizing, the body is reduced to a biological organism, to a system of needs, to an energy field or to a presentational self.

In an attempt to recover the concrete, living subject in a non-dualistic and non-reductionistic manner, a number of researchers have begun to turn their attention to the work of discourse theorists, primarily to M. Foucault. Although Foucault's work can illuminate how subjects' bodies have been socially constituted, a fundamental conflict exists between Foucault's project and the kind of theoretical work that a deeper understanding of the relentless pursuit of thinness would necessitate.

This conflict exists because, as Foucault (1980) states "... we must rid ourselves of the constituting subject, rid ourselves of the subject itself, which is to say arrive at an analysis which can account for the subject within an historical account" (p. 117). Foucault's archaeology rejects any recourse to the subject, to consciousness and to meaning-giving existence. Individuals, even collectively, don't make or move history. In Foucault's accounts, the individual is reduced to a parrot (Turner 1984) and to a "mere bearer of social relations" (Smith 1986, 4). People are either passive or not actually present, even in Foucault's discussions of power (Fine 1984). Foucault seems to assume that discourses have a general social effect, hence resistance escapes explanation (even problematization) in Foucault's writings (Turner 1984). In short, we could say that subjects (subjectivities) are artifacts of discursive practices for Foucault.

The authors of *Changing the Subject*, taking their lead from Foucault's work and, apparently, going beyond it, propose to account for subjectivity (and for differences among subjects) in terms of the "multiple positioning of subjectivity" (Henriques et al. 1984, 3). The subject is a particular place, an intersection of various discourses, which sets up a location and defines the individual's existence. The gist of the problem with Foucault's treatment of subjectivity and the body, as well as with the attempt to develop and apply Foucault's work in *Changing the Subject*, is that they either leave the question of the relationship between person (individual, subject) and world (specific situation) largely unanswered, or they answer this question inadequately. Foucault does not really have an answer; he solves the problem by purporting to get rid of the subject. The authors of *Changing the Subject* offer a pseudo-solution by merely deferring the question to another level of inquiry, one where we would be asking: What are the various discourses? How do they intersect? And why, in this particular manner, do they form this concrete subjectivity? Merely recording, describing and reshuffling the system of available discursive practices falls short of meeting this task. The subject is not a particular vacant place and nothing more. Equally, and for the same reason, we must challenge the archaeologist's statement that viewed from the proper distance everything turns out to be all surface, no depth, which Foucault suggested.

Work written from the sole perspective of discourse theory, as developed by Foucault, strikes me as being without depth and, despite claims of historicity, ahistorical and asituational. One possible reason for the apparent flatness and lack of historical basis in such work is the double reduction that the archaeologist seeks to perform — bracketing the claim for serious meaning in speech acts in addition to bracketing the truth value of the statement. Foucault, the same as any other social scientist, has a perspective that he cannot fully transcend. He was born into a world of meaning-giving existences that shaped him. The content of what is being said cannot be merely set aside; if all meaning could be set aside, it would be impossible to read any piece of work. Form stripped of all content is beyond my imagination. To provide pure description, as Foucault sought to do, is not a human possibility. Such attempts lead only to social science inquiries that lack reflexivity and leave untouched the problem of the subject-world relation.

To return to the body, it is inadequate to treat sexuality as merely a product of discourse. Sex is an aspect of being human, however it is expressed. Sex is not all relative. The body is not all relative and malleable. Torture, for example, depends on features of human bodies that cut across historical times and settings, even if the forms of torture have changed. Pain is a fundamental experience of bodies, and it is that universal human experience that co-creates the possibility of torture. The body is not only objectified and subjectified as a product of discursive practices (see Foucault 1979); rather, the body *is* both object and subject, as Merleau-Ponty explained. When we get rid of subjects who move history and when bodies are made relative, as we find them in Foucault's work, we end up with a position of utter pessimism. This position arises, in part, from Foucault's mistaken notion of pure descriptions that reveal the world as "all surface." What is not immediately visible in discourse, what cannot be taken at face value, does not seem to exist for Foucault. Social relations are not immediately visible. Nor is the interior, the felt, the "how" of our experiences and practices. The suffering women endure in trying to produce themselves as fashionably thin is largely a silent, quiet struggle. What women say and do around the same practices is often contradictory. Foucault's archaeology has nothing to say about these questions.

Feminist social scientists need to develop a way of thinking about the body that does not sever the intimate connections between person and world, that can address in its specificity the intertwining of gender, sexual orientation, cultural background, race, class, geographical region, age, education and the particular political economic structure in which women live. We need to understand how daily lived experience is constituted in its concrete situation and to analyze how social interactions and social relations are intertwined in our experiences of our bodies. We must begin with careful descriptions of everyday practices and resist leaping to the level of universal explanations prematurely. At the same time, we also must attempt to explicate social relations, the ever-present yet opaque horizon of all of our practices.

One crucial dimension of the task of interpreting anorexia is developing an adequate grasp of the body as both object and subject. Merleau-Ponty's phenomenology, and some of Foucault's studies of discourse, may prove to be fruitful contributions toward this project. But we must also guard against following too closely along the paths indicated by these authors. If we track the writings of Merleau-Ponty, we may learn how to describe and analyze individuals' experiences of their bodies in temporal terms, but we will not grasp as fully as necessary the social constitution of our bodily experiences. If we pursue the directions suggested by Foucault, we may gain valuable insight into how, through discursive practices, human bodies have been both objectified and subjectified. We will not, however, grasp these processes in their concreteness and immediacy, because in Foucault's writings the situated bodies of actual people tend to disappear. This last observation seems to apply to many writings inspired by discourse theory. Probyn's article on "The Anorexic Body" is a good example of this point. Although she calls for a return to the "everyday body" (Probyn 1987, 118), she does not describe the body at all. Writers working from a discourse theory perspective often appear to distance themselves from the body — to alter slightly the title of Michie's (1987) book, "The Flesh [is *only*] Made Word." The body, in its vitality, emotionality, sweat and trepidation is nowhere to be found (Corrigan 1988).

To grasp the body in its concrete and socially constituted vitality, we need a central category of the body, the dimension through which we will organize our descriptions and explications concerning the body. This organizing category may be activity viewed socially, historically and dialectically (Wertsch 1985; Lomov 1982; Leont'ev 1978). Since the body is always situated with others, in active interaction with subjects and objects in the world, and since it is in activity that self-other, inner-outer and subject-object come together in a unity (Davydov, Zinchenko & Talyzina 1983), activity appears uniquely suited to be the central category for investigating the body. It is a dynamic concept that necessitates a developmental, historical and dialectical approach grounded in praxis (Vygotsky 1978). Finally, the basic principles of a psychological analysis of activity — for example, object-relatedness as opposed to the stimulus principle, the active as opposed to the reactive principle, mediation as opposed to nonmediated associational relations, internalization and exter-nalization as opposed to socialization (see Asmolov 1987) — could be effective safeguards against the typical errors we find in psychological theorizing. While the difficulties should not be underestimated, it may be possible to incorporate some of the insights of feminist analyses, phenomenology and discourse theory within the framework of activity theory. We may then be able to develop an approach to the body both in its concreteness and historicity that would help us understand better — and act to prevent — the struggles of women in the relentless pursuit of thinness.

There is now a small but perhaps growing body of literature in Western psychology that tries to avoid many of the theoretical shortcomings I have critiqued. Frigga Haug and her colleagues have sought to understand "... women as active agents who are not simply stamped with the imprint of their given social relations, but who acquiesce in them and unconsciously parti-cipate in their formation" (Haug 1987, 25). This view of women as active agents underlies their analysis of sexuality as a form of socialization. These researchers asked, how sexuality itself is constituted as a "process that produces the insertion of women into, and subordination within, determinate social practices" (ibid., 33).

The work of Haug et al. brings us closer to formulating a social-historical approach to the gendered body. We can no longer view bodies as a "simple piece of nature" whose secrets we only need to dislodge in order to develop a "natural relationship with it" (ibid., 198), but rather must treat our bodies as unremittingly social and visible. They point to the rules, prohibitions, prescriptions and demands "whose influence takes effect from the outside inward," but these researchers also suggest that "within that rule-system, a relation of cause and effect from the inside outwards" exists as well (ibid., 198).

Their view of development is clearly one of a cultural process of transitions between interindividual and intraindividual activity. Similar to activity theorists (see Wertsch 1985), they recognize the mediating role of tools and signs in the development of our bodily experiences and practices. They seek to avoid treating individuals separately from the sociocultural settings of their lives, and, as we have seen, they refuse any unidirectional interpretations (solely from outside-in, or from inside-out) of development.

Haug et al. have understood that "There are not two different and originally contrary objects of investigation —body and thought — but only *one single* object, which is the *thinking body* of real [human beings]" (Ilyenkov 1977, 31). Haug et al. have insisted rightly that body, thought and effect are not separate. In fact, "It is around our bodies that we construct our identities; in so doing we simultaneously reproduce femininity within a particular social relation ..." (Haug, 119). However, they have not paid sufficient attention to the social-historical constitution of individual practices that they set out to investigate.

It is in the absence of a social-historical perspective that biological and psychological reductionistic explanations have been put forward for anorexia. The psychological explanations vary among authors, but all finally point to a single cause as the explanation of all anorexia. For example, where one author may maintain that all instances of anorexia have the rejection of femininity at their root, another may claim that the exaggerated striving for femininity is what it is all about. These explanations are not derived from concrete descriptions of actual women's lives in their social and historical situations. Although it is exceedingly difficult to explicate a set of practices and experiences of a person in their social constitution, this is the only viable starting point. Otherwise, we end up with speculative statements that are true for no one in particular and describe nothing about reality. Because the practices of women in the pursuit of thinness show great similarity, it does not mean that they can be reduced to a simple, common denominator located *within* the individuals.

Starting from actual practices of actual women in the pursuit of thinness, important questions emerge that some of the anorexia literature touches upon but fails to explore. One such question is that of class. Anorexia has been described as primarily an upper-class and upper-middle-class illness, even though many researchers have noted that the illness has become more prevalent among working-class women (Currie 1987). Most women I have known who were diagnosed anorexic (about thirty women) were not from the upper or upper-middle class. Neither were most of them Anglo-Saxon. They came from a number of different cultural backgrounds. What does this mean? Nearly all of the literature ignores the question of anorexic women's social class and cultural backgrounds.

We could begin searching for clues in a number of directions. One direction would be to take the word "disease" literally and say, "it has spread." How? Maybe genetic research will help us with the explanation, maybe we can attribute it to the cultural factor, or to some combination of the two. I do not advocate pursuing this line of inquiry. Another type of answer could rely on

the notion of patriarchy as the key to explaining the phenomenon: all women are subjected to male domination; men have
hated and/or envied women's bodies throughout history, and it is
this hostility to women's bodies that finds expression in anorexia.
This is what many theorists, whose work was discussed earlier,
have argued. This second explanation, however, evades the
question: why do we see more women from a wider range of
socio-economic and cultural backgrounds in Western societies
pursuing thinness? Is it because male hostility to women has
increased? Could it be the backlash against feminism — as a result
of an organized feminist movement that has been able to achieve
certain rights for certain groups of women, men have come to
hate and fear women more, and anorexia is men's increased
hatred internalized by women and manifested in the higher
incidence of anorexia? Such explanation would be both overly
simplistic and misleading.

Patriarchy as an explanation misses much about day-to-day
reality. We have seen that the women who were interviewed had
to be thin in order to obtain a job that allowed them to survive.
They also had to be thin to be considered healthy and to keep, and
be promoted in, a job. They needed to be attractive to enhance
their chances of finding and keeping the "right calibre" of man.
All of these reasons have to do with survival. Whose interest does
it serve that women have to obey the tyranny of slenderness? Is it
in men's, and in all men's interest in this society? Is it men, all
men, that discriminate among female employees or want women
to be dependent on their wages? Could it be that any man, if given
the opportunity, would keep women out of the work force, or pay
them at two-thirds or less of men's wages? And if so, in whose
interest would they do so, in their own or in someone else's
interest? Do most or all men want women to be ethereal, thin as a
twig, "dressed to a T"?

The patriarchal explanation would grant that it is not "all men"
who oppress and exploit women; there are always exceptions.
Nonetheless, it is men's interests on the whole that would be

served by women's objectification. This response, however, mistakes appearance for explanation. Objectively, it is not in men's but, rather, in our present political-economic system's interest to oppress and exploit women. This answer in no way denies that this society is misogynist and heterosexist. There is plenty of evidence in the data presented even in this one book that women have been treated as less than fully human — their bodies have been objectified, and they have been discriminated against. Men do much of the objectifying of women; most often men make decisions about hiring and firing, and those who marry decide who their wives will be. But the sum of individual men's practices does not account for the practices of women in the pursuit of thinness. Patriarchy understood as a discourse of domination is also insufficient to explain why among women, why among mostly white women, why in the "have" countries, and why now, the struggle exists to be fashionably thin?

The central piece missing from the feminist analyses that attribute the pursuit of thinness to patriarchy is class, defined in political-economic terms. This omission is not unique to feminist accounts of anorexia; a pervasive evasion of issues of class can be found in large segments of the feminist literature in general. The contemporary pursuit of thinness, however, cannot be understood without bringing into play capital, class and ideology. The most important ideology in the relentless pursuit of thinness is the belief that through individual hard work and determination one can be successful. One object of women's hard work which, potentially, is also a means of their success, is the body. In a sense, women have had some power through controlling their bodies. The recent emphasis on fitness, youth, health and thinness has played on this power through the body. Especially in the last decade, women have been given the message that their efforts in improving and perfecting their bodies would be rewarded by success in both their personal and professional lives.

These were the messages the interviewed women heard clearly in their teens and twenties. There was a certain basis in their social reality for believing that, indeed, women could succeed in careers previously closed to them. As a result of organized feminist struggles in this country and elsewhere in the western world, women have obtained rights and access to higher education, for example. Since the 1960s, a generation of women could grow up expecting that a life that involved valued paid work outside the home was a possibility for them. The double aspiration for marriage and career was evident in all of the interviews. We have seen that the requirements of preparing for each, however, often conflicted. The women were to be caring, compassionate and considerate, but also competitive and seeking to be number one. These conflicts point to real contradictions in the world. Some women have made gains in the area of employment, but the glorious image of the successful career woman has not been a realistic aspiration for most women. It simply could not be; a society cannot survive merely on the work of business people and professionals. Nevertheless, a generation of women has been raised with the expectation that they could have it all — a career and a happy family life.

The ideology of individualism is absolutely necessary for the functioning of a capitalist political-economic system. We are led daily, incessantly, to think that we, too, can make it. An entire popular-media system spreads the message and offers us endless advice about how to improve ourselves to enhance our chances for success. There are numerous courses, from how to trim the body in the smallest detail, through how to present ourselves at job interviews and how to be a millionaire. The ideology of individualism is a highly effective tool for dividing people. It operates in all walks of society — in schools, social service agencies, in the practices of medicine and other professions. We have seen it in the anorexic and non-anorexic split in the literature, as well as in the specific values that shaped the interviewed women's lives. The ideology of individualism works in part because there always are people who "make it." Only *how* they "make it," and how *few* make it, is not visible. We can point to examples of the ideal of success in careers for women. "If she could achieve X position, so could I! And, if I can't, it is my fault; I have not tried hard enough, wanted it badly enough, was not attractive enough or smart enough." We saw it laid bare in the interviews.

This ideology primarily serves capitalists', not men's, interests. Many men also benefit from it, however. Capitalists' and men's (at least short-term) interests intersect in patriarchal capitalism. It is mostly men who own and control capital; it is men who receive higher wages — and it is women who do most of the work. The benefits of capital accumulation accrue mostly to men, and to women only through men. This is what female supplication to catch the right man is based on. Capitalism needs new markets, cheap labour and a reserve army of unemployed. For these reasons, we are led to believe that we need new products, including clothes of the latest fashion. Those who do not have a well-paying job have not deserved one. Those who have no job at all are lazy. We call all of this equal opportunity, freedom and democracy. If certain practices contradict our experiences, we tend to gloss over them or explain those incidents in a way that does not disturb our beliefs in the essential truth of this social order. We are caught in contradictions, and at times they do become visible. From her own painful experiences Martha, for example, has become aware of many contradictions lived by women, including herself, and of some of the roots of these contradictions.

A set of these contradictions pertain specifically to capitalism's relation to women. At various times during and since World War Two, capitalism has needed women's labour in the work force. During the war, they were the factory and service workers. In the last twenty years, after the lull following the war years, increasing numbers of women have again returned to paid labour; in Canada today nearly sixty percent of women work in full-time or part-time jobs. Their pay cheques are often absolutely indispensable for providing their families' most basic needs. Women's employment in the labour force should not be looked at as a choice — as liberal ideology would have us believe. If patriarchal capitalism does not need women in the work force, it will not hire women. Women are the last hired and first fired, as we know well. If the system deems it too expensive to pay women the same wages as men, if equal pay does not bring the desired returns capitalists expect on expenditure, it will not pay women equally. There is nothing glorious about most women's jobs; they can hardly be said to provide opportunities for women's creative self-expression, nor do they pay well enough to compensate for the daily drudgery. Yet, in the current day-care debate in Canada, we hear women's work outside of the home being discussed as a "choice" and set up in opposition with "traditional family values." The liberal position in this debate is that "Women are people as well." Therefore, they should have the opportunity to opt for paid work — if they so desire.

For most women in North America and Western Europe, paid work is no more a choice than it is for men. Women, like immigrants of both sexes, have been blamed for unemployment among men and, more so in the United States than in Canada, for the higher rates of unemployment among Black men. Capitalists have exploited the growing economic hardship facing working people since the mid-1970s, by a massive ideological offensive aimed at dividing the working class (Waters 1986). The capitalist discourse has given its full support to the glorification of the family and to fostering guilt among women working outside the home. Mothers working in paid jobs have been pitted against those staying in the home; we hear this hostility echoed in the current day-care debate. Men have been pitted against women in trade unions and elsewhere.

These developments are not without their contradictions. Once women enter the paid labour force, they develop a consciousness of themselves as workers. They ask for and then demand rights of their own. Waters (1986) notes that women in full-time unionized industrial jobs are in the best position to resist the ideological offensive aimed at dividing the working class. They are less dependent on men, more self-confident and more politically conscious of themselves as working class than are women who labour in other sectors of the economy. They can see that not all men need to curtail their rights but only those men who are in a position to benefit from their exploitation through control of capital. They can see that it is primarily in capitalism's interest to try to force them back to their "true place" — family and home.

As a result of the recession that started in the mid-1970s, many middle-class families have also begun to experience increasing hardship. Due to the strength of capitalist ideology, however, instead of recognizing that their objective alliance was with the working class, many of them have pulled more toward right-wing politics. Simultaneously, the employers and the capitalist media have again been instrumental in weakening the women's movement. Feminism has been presented either as a preoccupation of white upper- and middle-class women — thus further severing whatever ties existed with working-class women, Women of Colour, Black women, aboriginal, immigrant and refugee women — or laced through with massive doses of homophobia, labelled a "lesbian plot," which resulted in splitting heterosexual and homosexual women.

This presentation of feminism by the media has played on some real conflicts that have existed among women, conflicts on whose roots women often disagree. The disagreement reflects, in part, objective differences that exist among women due to the intersection of their class location, race and sexual orientation. White anglophone feminists, as a recent conference in Toronto on "Women and the State" amply illustrated, have not dealt adequately with the issue of race and cultural difference (Feb. 1987, at Ontario Institute for Studies in Education). What has not been as visible as it should be is that at the heart of the conflicts among feminists, as in the rest of society, is an imperialist capitalist political-economic system that serves the interests of its ruling class. It is in the interest of capitalism to homogenize workers — to treat them as if they were all the same, *regardless of their sex and race*. For example, giving women certain benefits such as providing affordable day-care — because most of them are mothers as well as workers —would only increase labour costs (decrease profits). Offering language training to recent non-English or non-French speaking immigrants is also a cost capitalists do not want to incur. Barring lesbian and gay couples from obtaining family health coverage is another cost-saving measure. Selling the white images of attractiveness to Women of Colour and Black women, on the other hand, boosts profits.

But, when it suits capitalism's purposes, it seeks to divide people along lines of racial, cultural and sexual difference. It then pits men against women, white people against people of colour, Canadian-born against immigrant, younger against older, skilled against unskilled, employed against unemployed. Women, immigrants, Black people and people of colour end up with lower wages. Care is taken, however, that (on average) the wages are not so low that most people are unable to buy the consumer goods — the market must not shrink. We hear almost daily in Canada that the country needs more workers and consumers. Many people have argued that immigration quotas should be raised. Especially in metropolitan areas such as Toronto, a large portion of the population is neither white nor born in Canada. Immigrant Women of Colour, Black immigrant women and white immigrant women have begun to organize to obtain rights to work, education and other social and legal services. They have joined with the Native Indian peoples with Canadian-born and raised Women of Colour and Black women and men. Even though systemic racism, the practices of immigration, class differences and sexism divide us, even though our differences have been exploited by capitalism, it is also true that for its functioning this political-economic system needs us all — as workers and women. And, because we are all needed, we cannot be fully ignored. Capitalism is, in its effect, contradictory.

These are some of the issues at the root of the conflicts among women. A few women — mostly white upper- and middle-class women — are anxious to protect their privileges. Some women continue to deny — or do not (wish to) perceive — that racial, cultural and class differences do exist. Some women continue to speak about "sisterhood," without recognizing differences among women, without seeing that systemic racial, cultural, class and sexual differences are real obstacles to sisterhood. It may be in part because "as women, we have been taught to either ignore our differences, or view them as causes for separation and suspicion, rather than as forces for change" (Lorde 1984, 112). I fully agree with Audre Lorde when she says, yes, "... there are very real differences between us of race, age and sex" — and, I would add, class. She continues,

> But it is not those differences between us that are separating us. It is rather our refusal to recognize those differences, and to examine the distortions which result from our misnaming them and their effects upon human behavior and expectation. (p. 115)

The tragedy of the situation is that many women whose objective interests position them with *all* oppressed and exploited women continue to believe in the myth of individual success and happiness, as defined by ruling-class ideology and described in media discourse. This is the myth to which, as we have seen, women in the relentless pursuit of thinness have fallen victim.

At one level, women's struggles to be thin pursue a particular image of femininity. Women's striving to approximate the current ideal feminine body reflects accurately the demands they have faced in their immediate situations. Their aspiration to be attractively thin is consistent with many of the requirements made of them. Women's livelihood and their sense of self-worth has depended on their success or failure in producing a fashionable body. We must note, however, that the women also wanted to be feminine according to the prescribed ideal. This very aspiration has literally endangered the lives of many. To the extent that a few of the women have managed to approximate the ideal, they may have been able to achieve a certain measure of success. A few may have obtained a better paying job, or a "higher calibre" of man or both. Whether they succeeded or not in achieving the desired goal, however, their own work to produce themselves as attractively feminine has reinforced their objectification and systematic oppression.

To the extent that women's practices concerning their bodies and their relationships with others have conformed to the prescription of femininity, women have participated in strengthening the ideological offensive against themselves. The very practice of the relentless pursuit of thinness, then, is caught up in a contradiction. We must be clear, however, that it is not only women who have been labelled anorexic or bulimic who live in this contradictory situation; to a degree varying with our particular class, racial, cultural and sexual location, we are all caught up in the same contradiction. When we "put on our face," select matching earrings or wear "conservative clothes" for a job interview and, once at the interview, allow others to relate to us mainly as female bodies, our practices do not differ in essence from those of so-called anorexic women. Every such instance fuels discrimination against all women.

What are we going to do about this contradictory situation? If we buy into the prescriptions of femininity, in the short run a few of us may achieve certain individual gains. In the long run, however, we have effectively contributed to perpetuating situations that further oppress and exploit the majority of women in this society, including ourselves.

The contradictions that the relentless pursuit of thinness point to are not about whether women (or men, for that matter) should try to improve their appearance and make themselves attractive. The issue is not one of "to be or not to be attractive." We do not have to envision a world in which we will all look alike, dressed the same way, with identical hair-styles, deprived of any sensual and sexual expression. We do not have to extinguish our desire for variety, self-expression and the enjoyment of things beautiful. The point is that, in our society, fashion, with its entire prescription of the life-style to emulate, propagates classist, racist and heterosexist images of beauty that are defined outside and in conflict with the interests of the majority of women.

What are we to do, then, to prevent the practices of the relentless pursuit of thinness and other pursuits that contribute to the oppression, objectification and exploitation of women? The answers are contained in examining what has given rise to the *possibility and necessity* of such practices. It is unequivocal that women's situations must change. To transform women's lives so that we will not damage our own bodies in attempts to conform to an ideal, it is necessary to change the present social-political-economic system and the dominant culture — to overthrow patriarchal capitalism. This requires political, educational and ideological work. It requires critical analysis and, based on that analysis, organizing for social change. Part of the change must be full employment, with everyone receiving a liveable wage — to eliminate women's economic dependence on men. As the examples of socialist countries demonstrate, social-political-economic change alone will not liberate women. It is necessary to break down sexist attitudes and practices, to work consistently on an ideological and educational level, to alter the ways that women and men relate to each other on a daily basis. In this work it is important to emphasize the value of collective action and to challenge the tenets of liberal individualism.

Throughout this book much has been said about the popular media's treatment of women. Efforts must continue to fight the media's (hetero)sexist, racist, classist and ageist portrayal of women. We must challenge the images of health and thinness, demand truthful information about health, call for the regulation of weight-loss and fitness centres. As feminists, we must also examine our *own* pursuits of a thin, youthful and "healthy" body. We need to continue our fight for equal pay for work of equal value, for the deghettoization of women's jobs, for more educational, training and retraining opportunities. The struggle against sexism, sexual harassment and the legal system that continues to treat rape as woman's fault must go on. We must build solidarity among all women and all oppressed and exploited peoples. We must see ourselves and other women as active agents who —especially when we work together — can and do make a difference in the world. We have power; we need to use it more.

We must also pay more attention to the education girls — and boys — receive from their earliest age. We must produce and demand nonsexist and nonracist educational materials.

We need to call for more and accessible treatment facilities for women who have dieted, binged and purged. Treatment should be provided free of charge, by qualified persons who understand and are willing to challenge the social construction of femininity.

In this book I have wanted to show at least a few of the pieces that make up the social relations in which women live whose pursuit of thinness we call either "healthy" or "sick." I wanted the figure of the anorexic or bulimic woman to recede into the background and to bring some of the horizons to the fore. Once these women have been called "anorexic" or "bulimic," it is all too easy, despite our best efforts, to lose sight of the social dimensions and treat these women as if their problems were, in the last analysis, *individual* problems. They are not. Mental health professionals need to change the way they understand individual development. They need to extend the walls of their offices, clinics and hospitals, and recognize thoroughly that they are not dealing with personal problems. We must stop talking about the weak, vulnerable or otherwise deficient personality of the anorexic, and begin to acknowledge openly that their experiences and practices point to conflicts and contradictions that are *all of our problems*. When one of them says, "I am so busy thinking about food and my weight that I have no time to become interested in anything else," this woman speaks a piece of the truth of millions of North American women. She also speaks the words others of us cannot allow ourselves to pronounce. These women open spaces for us to ask questions, not only about how they, individually, ended up where they are, but also — and perhaps more importantly — about how thinness became a possible pursuit, and, for some women, the sole pursuit in life.

BIBLIOGRAPHY

Asmolov, A. 1987. Basic Principles of Psychological Analysis in the Theory of Activity. *Soviet Psychology* 1:78-102.

Baker, M. 1985. *"What Will Tomorrow Bring?..." A Study of the Aspirations of Adolescent Women.* Ottawa: Canadian Advisory Council on the Status of Women.

Bales, J. 1984, October. Garner: Social Pressures Influence Eating Disorders. *APA Monitor*, Oct., 16.

Barthes, Rolland. 1982. Encore le corps. *Critique*, 38. (Unpublished trans. D. Welsh.)

Berger, P., and T. Luckmann. 1967. *The Social Construction of Reality.* New York: Doubleday.

Berkow, R., ed. 1982. *The Merck Manual of Diagnosis and Therapy.* 14th ed. Rahway: Merck Sharp and Dohme.

Binswanger, L. 1958. The Case of Ellen West. In *Existence.* ed. R. May, E. Angel and H. Ellenberger. New York: Basic Books, 267-364.

Boone O'Neill, C. 1982. *Starving for Attention.* New York: Continuum.

Bors, D., and E. Szekely. 1981. Psychotherapy and the Building of a More Humanistic Society. Unpublished paper.

Boskind-Lodahl, M. 1976. Cinderella's Stepsisters Revisited: A Feminist Perspective on Anorexia Nervosa and Bulimia. *Signs* 2:342-56.

Boskind-White, M., and W. White. 1983. *Bulimarexia: The Binge/Purge Cycle.* New York: Norton.

Brothers, J. 1975. *Better Than Ever.* New York: Simon & Schuster.

Brown, L. 1985. Women, Weight and Power: Feminist Theoretical and Therapeutic Issues. *Women & Therapy* 1:61-71.

Brown, C. and D. Forgay. 1987. An Uncertain Well-being: Weight Control and Self-control. *Healthsharing*, (Winter):11-15.

Brownmiller, S. 1984. *Femininity.* New York: Simon & Schuster.

Bruch, H. 1979. *The Golden Cage.* Toronto: Random House.

Buhrich, N. 1981. Frequency of Presentation of Anorexia Nervosa in Malaysia. *Australian and New Zealand Journal of Psychiatry* 1:153-55.

Caskey, N. 1986. Interpreting Anorexia Nervosa. In *The Female Body in Western Culture*, ed. S. Suleiman. Cambridge, Mass.: Harvard Univ. Press, 175-189.

Casper, B., and E. Davis. 1980. Bulimia: Its Incidence and Clinical Importance in Patients with Anorexia Nervosa. *Archives of General Psychiatry* 37:1030-35.

Chernin, K. 1981. *The Obsession: Reflections on the Tyranny of Slenderness.* New York: Harper & Row.

Cline, S., and D. Spender. 1987. *Reflecting Men — At Twice Their Natural Size.* London: Andre Deutsch.

Corrigan, P. 1988. The body of intellectuals/the intellectuals' body (remarks for Roland). *Sociological Review* 2:368-80.

Coward, R. 1985. *Female Desire.* London: Granada.

Corner, Virginia. 1988. In search of a healthy body, mind and spirit. *The Toronto Star*, 9 Jan., C21.

Corner, Virginia. 1988. Great legs. *The Toronto Star*, 1 Jan., G1, G5.

Crisp, A., R. Palmer and R. Kalucy. 1976. How Common is Anorexia Nervosa? A Prevalence Study. *British Journal of Psychiatry*, no. 218, 549-54.

Currie, D. n.d. Women's Liberation and Women's Mental Health: Toward a Political Economy of Eating Disorders. Unpublished paper.

Darrow, W. 1970. *I'm Glad I'm a Boy! I'm Glad I'm a Girl!.* New York: Windmill.

Davydov, V., P. Zinchenko and N. Talyzina. 1983. The Problem of Activity in the Works of A. N. Leont'ev. *Soviet Psychology* 4:55-91.

de Beauvoir, S. 1961. *The Second Sex.* Trans. and ed. H.M. Parshley. New York: Bantam.

Delphy, C. 1984. *Close to Home.* Amherst: Univ. of Massachusetts Press.

Diamond, N. 1985. This Is the Feminist Issue. *Feminist Review* 1:45-65.

Dineen, J. 1987. Anorexia: The 'desperate need' for help. *The Toronto Star*, 17 March, B1-B2.

Dunn, P., and P. Ondercin. 1981. Personality Variables Related to Compulsive Eating in College Women. *Journal of Clinical Psychology* 1(37):43-49.

Dworkin, A. 1974. *Woman Hating.* New York: Dutton.

Dworkin, A. 1983. *Right-Wing Women.* New York: Putnam.

Dyer, G. 1982. *Advertising as Communication.* New York: Methuen.

Ehrenreich, B. 1984. *The Hearts of Men.* New York: Doubleday.

Enoch, Joan E. 1987. The Changing Role of Women and its Impact on Eating Disorders. *The Renfrew Perspective*, Fall.

Ewen, S. 1976. *Captains of Consciousness*. Toronto: McGraw-Hill.

Fadiman, A. 1982. Treating the emotions: The skeleton at the feast, a study of anorexia nervosa. *Life Magazine*, Feb., 63-66, 68, 70, 74, 76.

Faludi, S. 1988. Miss Teen Covina's Revenge. *Mother Jones*, April, 32-34, 52-55.

Fay, B. 1987. *Critical Social Science*. Ithaca, N.Y.: Cornell Univ. Press.

Fenwick, S. 1880. *On Atrophy of the Stomach and on the Nervous Affections of the Digestive Organs*. Churchill: London.

Ferguson, M. 1983. *Forever Feminine*. London: Heinemann.

Fine, B. 1984. *Democracy and the Rule of Law*. London: Pluto.

Fishburn, K. 1982. *Women in Popular Culture*. Westport, Conn.: Greenwood.

Fonda, J. 1983. *Jane Fonda Workout Book*. London: Penguin.

Foucault, M. 1979. *Discipline and Punish*. Trans. A. Sheridan. New York: Vintage.

Foucault, M. 1980. *Power/Knowledge*. Trans. C. Gordon, L. Marshall, J. Mepham and K. Soper. New York: Pantheon.

Foucault, M. 1985. *The Use of Pleasure*. Vol. 2, *The History of Sexuality*. Trans. R. Hurley. New York: Vintage.

Freedman, A., H. Kaplan and B. Sadock. 1972. *Modern Synopsis of Comprehensive Textbook of Psychiatry*. Baltimore: Williams and Wilkins.

Friday, Nancy. 1977. *My Mother/Myself*. New York: Dell.

Friedan, Betty. 1974. *The Feminine Mystique*. New York: Dell.

Friedman, M. 1985. Bulimia. *Women & Therapy* 2:63-69.

Fromm, E. 1955. *The Sane Society*. Greenwich, Conn.: Fawcett.

Garfinkel, P. 1981. Some Recent Observations on the Pathogenesis of Anorexia Nervosa. *Canadian Journal of Psychiatry* 6:218-23.

Garfinkel, P., and D. Garner. 1982. *Anorexia Nervosa: A Multidimensional Perspective*. New York: Brunner-Mazel.

Garfinkel, P., H. Moldofsky and D. Garner. 1980. The Heterogeneity of Anorexia Nervosa: Bulimia as a Distinct Subgroup. *Archives of General Psychiatry*, no. 37, 1036-40.

Garner, David. 1983a. Is Anorexia Nervosa Overidentified?. Psychiatric Grand Rounds, Sunnybrook Medical Centre, Toronto. 21 Oct.

Garner, David. 1983b. The Sociocultural Epidemic of Eating Disorders. *Health News Digest* [Toronto], March-April, 2-3.

Garner, David. 1983c. Anorexia Nervosa and Bulimia. Professional Development Day, Nursing, Toronto General Hospital, Toronto. 23 Nov.

Garner, D., and P. Garfinkel. 1980. Sociocultural Factors in the Development of Anorexia Nervosa. *Psychological Medicine* 10:647-57.

Garner, D., P. Garfinkel, D. Schwartz and M. Thompson. 1980. Cultural Expectations of Thinness Among Women. *Psychological Reports*, no. 47, 483-91.

Halmi, K. 1983. Anorexia Nervosa and Bulimia. *Psychosomatic Illness Review* 2:111-29.

Halmi, K., J. Falk and E. Schwartz. 1981. Binge Eating and Vomiting: A Survey of the College Population. *Psychological Medicine*, no. 11, 697-706.

Harkaway, J. 1987. *Eating Disorders*. Rockville, Md: Aspen.

Haug, Frigga. 1987. Daydreams. *New Left Review*, no. 162.

Haug, Frigga, Ed. 1987. *Female Sexualization*. London: Verso.

Henriques, J., W. Hollway, C. Urwin, C. Venn and V. Walkerdine. (1984). *Changing the Subject*. London: Methuen.

Holub, Kathy. 1987. Sculpting down to size. *The Toronto Star*, 7 Dec., C1-C2.

Horton, M. 1985. Health club romances: for the love or sweat of it?. *Slimmer*, Aug., 32-33.

Howe, Florence. 1976. The Education of Women. In *And Jill Came Tumbling After: Sexism in American Education*, Ed. Judith Stacey, Susan Béreaud and Joan Daniels. New York: Dell, 64-75.

Ideas: The cult of the body. 1983. CBC Radio, 2-23 Feb., 4-ID-022. Host: Kevin Marsh.

Ideas: Just Desserts — Women and food. 1987. CBC Radio, 19-26 Oct., 4ID7-231. Host: Lister Sinclair.

Ilyenkov, E. 1977. *Dialectical Logic*. Moscow: Progress.

Janos, J. 1985. Jane Fonda: Finding her Golden Pond. *Cosmopolitan*, Jan.

Johnson, A. 1987. The fat of the land. *The Globe and Mail*, May 1987, Report on Business.

Kafka, F. 1971. A Hunger Artist. In *Franz Kafka: The Complete Short Stories*, ed. N. Glatzer, Willa Muir and Edwin Muir. New York: Schocken, 268-77.

Keeton, K. 1986. First Word. *Omni*, Jan., 1.

Keys, A., J. Brozek, A. Henschel, O. Mickelsen and H. Taylor. 1950. *The Biology of Human Starvation*. Minneapolis: Univ. of Minnesota Press.

Kiernan, T. 1983. *Jane Fonda: Heroine for Our Time*. New York: Berkley.

Kipnis, L. 1985. *Ecstasy Unlimited: The Interpretation of Sex and Capital*. (Video).

Koch, S. 1959. *Psychology: The Study of a Science*. New York: McGraw-Hill.

Larrick, N., and E. Merriam. 1973. *Male and Female Under 18*. New York: Avon.

Lazerson, J. 1982. Voices of Bulimia: Experiences in Integrated Psychotherapy. Unpublished paper.

Leont'ev, A. 1978. *Activity, Consciousness and Personality*. Englewood Cliffs, N.J.: Prentice-Hall.

Levenkron, S. 1978. *The Best Little Girl in the World*. New York: Warner.

Levenkron, S. 1982. *Treating and Overcoming Anorexia Nervosa*. New York: Warner.

Liu, A. 1978. *Solitaire*. New York: Harper & Row.

Lomov, B. 1982. The Problem of Activity in Psychology. *Soviet Psychology* 1:55-91.

Lorde, A. 1984. *Sister Outsider*. Trumansburg, N.Y.: Crossing Press.

Loren, S. 1984. *Women and Beauty*. London: Aurum.

Lowe, M. 1982. Social Bodies: The Interaction of Culture and Women's Biology. In *Biological Woman: The Convenient Myth*, Ed. R. Hubbard, M. Henifin and B. Fried. Cambridge, Mass.: Schenkman, 91-116.

McRobbie, A. 1978. Jackie: An ideology of adolescent femininity. *Working Papers in Cultural Studies*, SP53, Birmingham Centre for Contemporary Cultural Studies.

Merleau-Ponty, M. 1962. *Phenomenology of Perception*. London: Routledge & Kegan Paul.

Merleau-Ponty, M. 1963. *The Structure of Behavior*. Boston: Beacon.

Michie, H. 1987. *The Flesh Made Word: Female Figures and Women's Bodies*. New York: Oxford Univ. Press.

Millman, M. 1980. *Such a Pretty Face*. New York: Berkley.

Minuchin, S., B. Rosman and L. Gailer, eds. 1978. *Psychosomatic Families: Anorexia Nervosa in Context*. Cambridge, Mass.: Harvard Univ. Press.

Morris, Bernadine. 1985. New slender shapes. *Toronto Globe and Mail*. Dec. 17.

Morris, B. 1985. The Phenomenon of Anorexia Nervosa: A Feminist Perspective. *Feminist Issues* 2:89-99.

Nopper, S., and J. Harley. 1986. How society's obsession with thinness is consuming women. *HERizons*, Oct.-Nov., 24-42.

Nunes, M., and D. White. 1973. *The Lace Ghetto*. Toronto: new.

O'Neill, J. 1985. *Five Bodies*. Ithaca, N.Y.: Cornell Univ. Press.

Orbach, Suzy. 1980. *Fat Is a Feminist Issue*. New York: Berkley.

Orbach, Suzy. 1986. *Hunger Strike*. New York: Norton.

Palazzoli, M. 1974. *Anorexia Nervosa*. London: Chaucer.

Palmer, R. 1983. *Anorexia Nervosa*. Harmondsworth, Eng.: Penguin.

Polivy, J., and P. Herman. 1985. Dieting and Binging. *American Psychologist* 2:193-201.

Pope, H., and J. Hudson. 1985. *New Hope for Binge Eaters*. New York: Harper & Row.

Pope, H., J. Hudson and D. Yugelun-Todd. 1984. Anorexia Nervosa and Bulimia Among 300 Suburban Women Shoppers. *American Journal of Psychiatry* 2:292-94.

Pope, H., et al. 1984. Prevalence of Anorexia Nervosa and Bulimia in Three Student Populations. *International Journal of Eating Disorders* 3:45-51.

Probyn, E. 1987. The Anorexic Body. *Canadian Journal of Political and Social Theory* 1-2:111-19.

Rose, S., L. Kamin and R. Lewontin. 1984. *Not in Our Genes: Biology, Ideology and Human Nature*. Harmondsworth, Eng.: Penguin.

Rost, W., M. Neuhaus and I. Florin. 1982. Bulimia Nervosa: Sex Role Attitude, Sex Role Behavior, and Sex Role Related Locus of Control in Bulimarexic Women. *Journal of Psychosomatic Research* 4(26):403-08.

Ryan, W. 1971. *Blaming the Victim*. New York: Vintage.

Sartre, J.-P. 1963. *Search for Method*. New York: Random House.

Sayers, J. 1986. *Sexual Contradictions*. London: Tavistock.

Schwartz, D., M. Thompson and C. Johnson. 1982. Anorexia Nervosa and Bulimia: The Sociocultural Context. *International Journal of Eating Disorders* 1:20-36.

Schwartz, H. 1986. *Never Satisfied*. New York: Free.

Scotton, Lindsay. 1984. Superfit! Why we choose to get in shape. *The Toronto Star*, 21 April, M1, M9.

Sellers, P. 1984. Tracey's story. *Starweek Magazine [The Toronto Star]*, 6 July.

Silverstein, B. 1984. *Fed Up!*. Boston: South End.

Slopen, B. 1984. Going, going, gone. *Quill & Quire*, Feb.

Smith, D.E. 1974. The Ideological Practice of Sociology. *Catalyst* 1:39-54.

Smith, D.E. 1978. K Is Mentally Ill: The Anatomy of a Factual Account. *Sociology* 1:23-53.

Smith, D.E. 1984. Women, Class and Family. In *The Socialist Register 1983*, Ed. R. Milliband and J. Saville. London: Merlin.

Smith, D.E. 1986. Femininity as Discourse. Unpublished paper.

Sokol, A. 1985. Women body builders train hard. *The Toronto Star*, 20 March, F4.

Spelman, E. 1982. Woman as Body: Ancient and Contemporary Views. *Feminist Studies* 1:109-31.

Spender, D. 1980. *Man Made Language*. London: Routledge & Kegan Paul.

Squire, S. 1984. *The Slender Balance*. New York: Pinnacle.

Sternhell, C. 1985. Some of us will always be fat but fat can be fit. *Ms.*, May.

Stoppard, J. 1988. Depression in Women: Psychological Disorder or Social Problem?. *Atlantis*, Fall.

Strober, M. 1981. A Comparative Analysis of Personality Organization in Juvenile Anorexia Nervosa. *Journal of Youth and Adolescence* 4:285-95.

Strupp, H. 1974. Some Observations on the Fallacy of Value-Free Psychotherapy and the Empty Organism. *Journal of Abnormal Psychology* 2:285-95.

Sugarman, A., D. Quinlan and L. Devenis. 1982. Ego Boundary Disturbance in Anorexia Nervosa: Preliminary Findings. *Journal of Personality Assessment* 5:455-61.

Sweet, Lois. 1988. Group fights our Obsession with thinness. *The Toronto Star*, 24 Feb., D1.

Szekely, E. 1987. Society, Ideology and the Relentless Pursuit of Thinness. *Practice* 3:34-48.

Szekely, E., and N. Morris. 1986. Anorexia Nervosa: A Psychometric Investigation of Hospitalized Patients. Unpublished paper.

Szyrynski, V. 1973. Anorexia Nervosa and Psychotherapy. *American Journal of Psychotherapy*, 2: 492-505.

Thoma, H. 1967. *Anorexia Nervosa*. New York: International Universities Press.

Turner, B. 1984. *The Body and Society*. Oxford: Basil Blackwell.

Turner, Janice. 1988. The business of dieting. *The Toronto Star*, 28 Jan., L1, L4.

Vincent, L. 1981. *Competing with the Sylph*. New York: Berkley.

Vygotsky, L. 1978. *Mind in Society*. Cambridge, Mass.: Harvard Univ. Press.

Walkerdine, V. 1984. Some Day My Prince Will Come. In *Gender and Generation*, Ed. A. McRobbie and M. Nava. London: Macmillan, 162-84.

Waters, M. 1986. The Capitalist Ideological Offensive Against Women Today. In *Cosmetics, Fashion and the Exploitation of Women*, Ed. J. Hansen and E. Reed. New York: Pathfinder, 3-28.

Wertsch, J. 1985. *Vygotsky and the Social Formation of the Mind*. Cambridge, Mass.: Harvard Univ. Press.

Wilson, S. 1976. The Changing Image of Women in Canadian Mass Circulating Magazines, 1930-1970. CRIAW Conference, Halifax. Nov. Printed 1977. *Atlantis* 2 (2, Pt. II), 33-44.

Woodman, M. 1980. *The Owl Was a Baker's Daughter.* Toronto: Inner City Books, 1980.

Woodward, H. 1926. *Through Many Windows.* New York.

Wooley, O., and S. Wooley. 1982. The Beverly Hills Eating Disorder: The Mass Marketing of Anorexia Nervosa. *International Journal of Eating Disorders* 3:57-69.

Yager, J. 1982. Family Issues in the Pathogenesis of Anorexia Nervosa. *Psychosomatic Medicine* 1:43-59.

Zarzour, Kim. 1987a. Fat and feeling fine. *The Toronto Star*, 3 Dec.

Zarzour, Kim. 1987b. Take a sensible approach when it comes to dieting. *The Toronto Star*, 3 Dec, L1, L6.